Children's Prose Comprehension
research and practice

Edited by
Carol Minnick Santa
Kalispell Reading Project
School District #5
Kalispell, Montana

Bernard L. Hayes
Utah State University

For the IRA Studies and Research Committee

International Reading Association
800 Barksdale Road   Newark, Delaware 19711

Copyright 1981 by the
International Reading Association, Inc.

Library of Congress Cataloging in Publication Data
Main entry under title:

Children's prose comprehension

   Bibliography: p.
   CONTENTS: Baker, L. and Stein, N. The development of prose comprehension skills.—Levin, J. R. and Pressley, M. Improving children's prose comprehension.—Johnson, D.D. and Barrett, T.C. Prose comprehension.—[etc.]
   1. Reading comprehension—Addresses, essays, lectures.
I. Santa, Carol Minnick. II. Hayes, Bernard L.
III. International Reading Association. Studies and Research Committee.
LB1050.45.C46   372.4'1   80-21883
ISBN 0-87207-730-6

Contents

Foreword   v

1 Introduction   *Carol Minnick Santa* and *Bernard L. Hayes*

Review Chapters

7 The Development of Prose Comprehension Skills
   Linda Baker and *Nancy Stein*

44 Improving Children's Prose Comprehension: Selected Strategies
    that Seem to Succeed   *Joel R. Levin* and *Michael Pressley*

72 Prose Comprehension: A Descriptive Analysis of Instructional
    Practices   *Dale D. Johnson* and *Thomas C. Barrett*

Discussant Chapters

103 Can We Integrate Research and Instruction on Reading
     Comprehension?   *Thomas Trabasso*

117 A Retrospective Reaction to Prose Comprehension
     P. David Pearson

133 Research and the Reality of Reading
     Marjorie Seddon Johnson

Conclusion

157 Children's Reading Comprehension: A Final Word
     Carol Minnick Santa

References   171

The International Reading Association attempts, through its publications, to provide a forum for a wide spectrum of opinion on reading. This policy permits divergent viewpoints without assuming the endorsement of the Association.

Foreword

As this volume demonstrates, prose comprehension research is a topic that continues to receive a great deal of attention. It is impossible to pick up a research journal in education or psychology without seeing an article or two that mentions discourse analysis, text structure, schema theory, mathemagenics, or other prose comprehension topics. This does not mean that these research issues were not considered important in the past; it merely reflects the influence information processing theories have had on prose comprehension research in general and reading comprehension specifically.

However, with all the time and energy that have been devoted to this particular topic, one has to wonder whether research affects instruction. Or more specifically, is it realistic to assume that pedagogical strategies or materials development for classroom utilization should be predicated upon implications, suggestions, or recommendations emanating from basic and applied research? Often, the basic researcher, the applied researcher, and the classroom practitioner operate as semi-isolated elements within the educational community. For this reason, it is refreshing to see a monograph address a specific topic from an interdisciplinary perspective. All too frequently educators, psychologists, linguists, and sociologists do not attempt to discern how those operating at different levels (teacher, researcher, material developer) might benefit from one another. For example, do basic researchers have anything to offer classroom teachers or material developers in terms of how they might approach their specific areas of concern? Conversely, do classroom practitioners and material developers have recommendations that basic researchers would find useful?

While it is evident from this volume that researchers and practitioners are becoming more concerned with interdisciplinary issues, it is only a beginning. If classroom teachers are to view researchers in a less antagonistic perspective, and if the researcher is to develop research methodologies that are more consistent with educational practices, a more concerted effort at cooperation must be established. This monograph is evidence that the process has begun and, as Santa cogently points out in her concluding chapter, educators seem to be receptive to ideas and issues that psychologists raise and psychologists are likewise receptive to practical constraints and suggestions made by those in the classroom.

As Mark Twain once said about a man contemplating drinking a glass of water taken directly from the Missouri River, "Don't be so perplexed by its murky appearance. If you just let the glass sit for a half hour, the soil will sink to the bottom. Once this has taken place, both portions are useful. However," he admonished, "the natives do not separate the elements; they drink them as nature intended." I think Mark Twain's comments have some relevance to educators. While we may be able to separate the various components that are identified with comprehension processes, we must not lose sight of the natural milieu from which they came. This monograph certainly has not.

The International Reading Association, along with the editors and contributors to this volume, is to be commended for providing *Children's Prose Comprehension* for the reading profession.

CHARLES W. PETERS
Oakland Schools
Pontiac, Michigan

Introduction

Carol Minnick Santa
Kalispell Reading Project
School District No. 5
Kalispell, Montana
            and
Bernard L. Hayes
Utah State University

The present book was designed to provide an exchange of ideas about children's reading comprehension and to gather in a single volume the insights and perspectives of both educators and psychologists regarding the comprehension process. As editors of the volume, we invited several contributors to prepare review chapters designed to provide a summary of their discipline's concern with children's comprehension. We then attempted to stimulate an interdisciplinary exchange by inviting another set of experts to provide a critical response to the information presented in the review chapters. It was our hope that such a volume would prove informative to all educators and psychologists concerned with children's reading comprehension.

As editors of the present work, we carefully prepared a few comments to explain the present need for such an interdisciplinary look at comprehension. Fortunately, when all of the chapters were submitted, David Pearson had already written an excellent account of the resurgence of interest in comprehension in psychology and education. So, with gratitude to Pearson, we have included in our introduction his comments on the timeliness of an interdisciplinary effort:

Comprehension: An Idea Whose Time Has Come

Comprehension is an idea whose time has come. Teachers are concerned about it (witness the concern expressed about test scores which seem to decrease suddenly about grade four). Psychologists have finally given it their blessing (compare articles in a journal like the *Journal of Verbal Learning and Verbal Behavior* today versus a year ago). Reading educators have embraced it (until the last decade there were no reading texts primarily devoted to reading comprehension). Indeed, I doubt that a volume like this could have been written a decade ago.

The past decade has been exciting for those of us who began it with a commitment to understanding the comprehension process and finding ways to improve comprehension instruction. But we ask ourselves, Why now? Why not a decade ago? What has happened to allow comprehension issues to move to center stage in the reading arena? Several things.

First, psychology has escaped the grasp of behaviorism. From the decade of the twenties to the decade of the sixties, little appeared in the experimental psychology literature that dealt with unobservable or mentalistic phenomena. What could not be conveniently compartmentalized into stimuli and responses was not studied. Hence, reading comprehension, being both mentalistic and unobservable, did not get studied. By contrast, the seventies have witnessed a shift toward the study of cognitive processes within experimental psychology. Those of us in the reading field now have the field of cognitive psychology as a powerful ally in trying to unravel the mysteries of reading comprehension.

Second, reading educators have reached clearer consensus on issues of teaching word identification. In the early sixties, the contrasts between commercially available reading programs (especially at the early levels) were stark. These contrasts—for example, between the meaning emphasis basals and the code emphasis phonic and linguistic systems—reflected strong philosophical differences in underlying conceptualizations of the reading process. Those philosophical differences remain; however, the contrasts between commercially available programs are becoming fuzzy. The old look-say approaches have incorporated more code emphasis. Linguistic series have relented, too, and now allow pictures and comprehension questions even in the early readers. We seem to be headed toward a rather uniform eclecticism when it comes to issues of word identification. This may be an illusion, it may be unwarranted; nevertheless, it has freed up energy that can be devoted to issues of reading comprehension.

Third, there is a growing uneasiness among teachers and administrators that something unpleasant is occurring along about grade four. I have personally heard the following complaint from at least ten administrators or reading curriculum study groups: "We don't know why, but somehow our standardized test scores are fine until grade four. Then our mean scores start a slide that continues through junior high school, at least. It must be that we do a great job of teaching word identification skills but a lousy job of teaching comprehension skills." This concern is reflected in the kinds of help that schools are asking for in their requests for in-service. A decade ago, nothing seemed more popular than workshops on decoding and vocabulary games. Today, teachers want to know how children comprehend, why they fail to comprehend, and what to do with and for them when they fail.

Fourth, there seems to be an uncanny convergence toward issues of prose comprehension across many disciplines. Traditional linguists, sociolinguists, speech-art theorists, psychologists, computer scientists, and reading educators seem to be focusing their research efforts along a continuum that is bounded by the structure of text on one end and the structure of knowledge in the human mind at the other. Different lexicons and idioms still cloud communication between these groups of scholars. Even so, they all seem to be concerned with the same problem: the relationship between what we know and how we understand when we read.

In short, a book such as this is possible today because we have finally marshalled the motivation, the commitment, the human resources, and the understandings necessary to make a good start at understanding and improving children's reading comprehension. Underscore the words, *make a good start*. Neither this volume nor the scores of books, curriculum projects, research studies, and articles that will follow in the next decade will fully complete the task. Nonetheless, efforts like this one provide us with "great expectations" about what we will be able to accomplish in the near future in both the research laboratory and the classroom.

In organizing this volume, we had two goals in mind. First, we wanted to examine the development of reading comprehension at several levels from basic research through the teaching of comprehension. Second, we wanted the contributors, both research psychologists and reading educators, to interact with one another.

To satisfy our first objective, the present volume contains three literature reviews representing different levels of concern with comprehension. Our first review chapter covers basic research on the development of prose comprehension. The second chapter is somewhat more applied in that it focuses on experimental manipulations designed to promote children's comprehension. The third chapter, written by educators, contains information about successful instructional materials and practices used for teaching children to comprehend.

To satisfy our second objective, we offered an opportunity for an exchange of ideas by including three discussant chapters. The discussants, experts in at least one of the three chapter topics, provide a critical commentary on all of the review chapters with their main focus being one of integration and evaluation. While each discussant was assigned to review one chapter in depth, their comments on all three review chapters provide an interdisciplinary perspective.

In hope of enticing the reader to go beyond these introductory pages, let us now take a moment to summarize briefly the content of each chapter. In the first review chapter, Linda Baker and Nancy Stein present a very thoughtful and thorough discussion of current research on the development of prose comprehension skills. After discussing some problems in measuring comprehension, they present research organized around various skill areas: identifying the main ideas, understanding logical structure, making inferences, and using higher order structures such as story grammars. Throughout, the authors evaluate the state of the art by noting limitations of present research and by making suggestions for further study. In addition, they have made an effort to relate experimental work with educational practice.

Joel Levin and Michael Pressley, authors of the second chapter, review research about strategies which seemingly improve children's comprehension. They provide a model which compartmentalizes comprehension into strategies used by the reader (processor-dependent) or writer (prose-dependent) of materials. They, in turn, discuss strategies according to whether they occur before a passage is read (stage-setting strategy) or during actual reading (storage/retrieval strategy). Based on this framework, they present a lively discussion of such stage setting activities as advance organizers, or verbal and pictorial aids to comprehension. They also describe experiments demonstrating the vital role of experiential background in comprehension. From here, the authors discuss the types of storage/retrieval strategies brought into play during actual reading. They particularly emphasize the importance of visual illustrations as a device for improving comprehension. They also note several procedures useful for inducing students to organize and elaborate information while reading.

The third review chapter, written by Dale Johnson and Thomas Barrett, differs from the other two by its focus on educational practice. The authors begin by organizing comprehension skills into a taxonomy of seventeen tasks, and based upon this taxonomy evaluate selected third and fifth grade instructional materials. They summarize which of these seventeen skills are actually included in typical basal readers and, as one might expect, there is considerable variability with some skills receiving quite lavish treatment while others are practically overlooked. They also evaluate selected professional textbooks on reading instruction and conclude with a discussion of currently emphasized strategies used by teachers in the classroom to promote comprehension.

Thomas Trabasso, the first of our discussants, comments primarily on the Baker and Stein chapter, but also provides an insightful evaluation of the other review chapters. He also presents an excellent description of one particular school system's program for teaching reading comprehension. Trabasso offers this program description to highlight the contrast between the richness of the applied problem of reading comprehension with the impoverished models currently offered by psychologists. He notes that for the psychologist, comprehension is practically synonymous with memory; whereas, for the educator, comprehension is a much more complex domain, left largely untapped by recall tasks. Trabasso also discusses problems inherent in measuring comprehension with recall tasks, and suggests that psychologists go into the classroom to determine what teachers do to promote and measure comprehension. On the other hand, he suggests that educators begin using some of psychology's analytic tools for operationalizing such notions as background knowledge, main ideas, causal relationships and factual recall.

David Pearson was primarily responsible for critiquing the Levin and Pressley chapter. In his commentary, he notes that research may presently have more implications for publishers than for teachers, but feels the Levin and Pressley chapter represents a "catalog of promising and partially successful ideas" which teachers might want to validate in their classrooms. In reviewing the Baker and Stein contribution, Pearson notes some problems with research on main ideas and clarifies several important issues regarding the relationship between prior knowledge and reading comprehension. With the Barrett and Johnson chapter, Pearson points out a number of difficulties in constructing taxonomies of comprehension skills and comments on the authors' examination of instructional materials and their description of teaching methodologies. Finally, Pearson outlines the role of research in educational practice and, in a "guarded" message to publishers and authors, he sets forth some tentative guidelines for writing instructional materials.

Marjorie Johnson, voicing the educator's point of view, begins her commentary with an historical overview of reading comprehension research. In discussing Johnson and Barrett's chapter, she notes that educators and researchers often have neglected self-directive aspects of reading. Teachers and researchers traditionally have examined situations where outside agents take charge of the child's comprehension. Johnson feels there should be a shift in focus to examine situations which create independent self-directed readers. In reviewing the research presented in the Baker and Stein and Levin and Pressley chapters, she notes that most investigators should examine issues within more realistic reading situations. Both researchers and educators need to consider the reader's motivation and purpose of reading as well as take more care in using material appropriate to task demands and reader ability. In sum, Johnson provides us with constructive suggestions for improving both our understanding and teaching of reading comprehension.

The Development of Prose Comprehension Skills

Linda Baker
University of Maryland at Baltimore
and
Nancy Stein
University of Illinois at Urbana-Champaign

In view of the tremendous role that reading plays in most of our lives, we know amazingly little about the processes involved in reading comprehension. Though this paucity of knowledge may seem surprising, it becomes more understandable when we consider how complex comprehension really is. Comprehension of prose, whether written or oral, involves considerably more than understanding the meanings of individual words and sentences; it also requires that one understand how the ideas expressed in one sentence are related to ideas expressed in other sentences. An even more critical component of comprehension is the knowledge that one brings to the reading situation; in fact, the same passage may be understood in different ways depending on a reader's background. Thus, comprehension involves a complex interplay between the reader and the material.

It is only within the past decade that comprehension has gained widespread attention as a domain of study. Most of the research has focused on adult subjects in order to investigate the comprehension process in mature readers. (See Goetz & Armbruster, in press, and Reder, 1978 for reviews of this literature.) Several of the adult findings have stimulated experiments on the development of comprehension, and these developmental experiments will be reviewed in this chapter. The main thrust of the research thus far has been to document the comprehension skills possessed by children of various ages and the changes these skills undergo with age. This information is clearly important to a developmental psychologist, but its value to a reading educator is more nebulous. The research demonstrates *when* one might expect certain skills to develop, but it does not provide much insight into *how* they develop. Though the latter is certainly a critical question to all those interested in comprehension, the research efforts are not yet sufficiently mature to provide the answers. Thus, many of the studies may seem of tangential relevance to reading comprehension instruction. Nevertheless, we feel that because the research has bearing on the development of comprehension, it is of practical value. We will discuss these practical implications in the concluding section of the chapter.

In searching for a framework within which to organize our review, we observed that most studies addressed specific skills that contribute to comprehension instead of treating comprehension as a global process. The four most commonly explored skills were identifying main ideas, understanding logical structures, making inferences, and using higher order knowledge structures (most studies have focused on knowledge about the structure of stories). A concern with these four skills is also apparent in comprehension instruction. Typical workbook exercises for beginning readers include finding main ideas, unscrambling sentences in a passage to make sense, making inferences about story characters, and making up or completing stories. Research relevant to each of these skills will be discussed in turn, but the classification is primarily an expository convenience. We are not suggesting that these are the only skills involved in comprehension nor that they should be studied or taught in isolation. In fact, we believe that such skills are highly interdependent in normal comprehension.

Some Preliminary Comments on Measuring Comprehension

One of the more difficult problems associated with comprehension research is the choice of an appropriate method for assessment. Just as no one is quite satisfied with existing reading comprehension tests in the schools, so no one is quite satisfied with current experimental methodology for testing comprehension. This problem has been discussed at length elsewhere (Carroll, 1972; Farr, 1969; Greeno, 1977), but a few comments are in order to acquaint the reader with the techniques used in the research we will be discussing. There are countless variations on the definition of comprehension and, needless to say, the way it is defined influences the way it is measured. Nevertheless, the different definitions share enough common features that comparisons among experiments are meaningful.

Virtually all of the measures of comprehension that experimenters have adopted impose some sort of memory demand on the subjects. Rather than testing for comprehension in the presence of the reading material (as do many standardized tests), experimenters typically present the material, remove it, and then test for memory. The most common memory tests are free recall, probed recall, and recognition. Free recall tests require the subject to produce everything that can be remembered about the material. Such tests are similar to essay questions students receive on exams. Probed recall tests require the subject to provide specific information about the material, and are often in the form of "wh" questions. These tests are analogous to short answer exam questions. Recognition tests require the subject to discriminate statements that are identical to or consistent with the studied passage from related alternatives. Such "objective" tests correspond to the multiple choice or true/false items often found on standardized tests.

The rationale for using memory tests as an index of comprehension is that poorly understood material will not be well-remembered (unless it is rotely memorized; i.e., many children can recite the Pledge of Allegiance but do not comprehend it). This rationale received empirical support in studies by Bransford and Johnson (1972) and Thorndyke (1977), where a close relationship was found between the amount of information recalled from a passage and ratings of its comprehensibility. However, one should be cautious in concluding that something has not been understood because it was not remembered. A reader may have good comprehension during reading, but may not be able to remember the material later. Moreover, memory tests of comprehension are plagued with the possibility of a production or response bias. That is, the index of comprehension is based only on the subjects' overt responses; it is possible that something will be comprehended at the time of reading, and remembered at the time of testing, but excluded in the subject's response. Suppose, for example, that you read a story about three little boys named Steve, Mike, and Alan. You are told that Steve is the oldest, Alan is the youngest, and Mike is wearing a blue shirt. On a recall test you might well state that Steve is the oldest and Alan the youngest. But you might leave out the inference that Mike's age is somewhere between that of Steve's and Alan's. You might have left this out because you thought it obvious, or perhaps because you thought your answer should include only explicitly stated information. Similarly, you might leave out the fact that Mike was wearing a blue shirt because, although you remembered it, the fact seemed trivial and not worth mentioning. As this example demonstrates, recall tests often provide a faulty index of comprehension, since subjects are free to decide how much and what information to include. This problem is better controlled in probed recall and recognition tests, but recognition tests introduce another bias problem associated with response criteria (Coombs, Dawes, & Tversky, 1970).

One way to circumvent the potential discrepancy between what the tester wants and what the reader recalls is to demand verbatim recall (i.e., asking the subject to recall the exact words of the passage). Most people agree that this is too stringent a requirement and so subjects are usually allowed to recall in their own words. However, experimenters often establish highly subjective criteria in scoring for "gist" recall. In view of this problem, several researchers have developed models for representing the semantic content of a passage (e.g., Crothers, 1972; Fredericksen, 1972; Kintsch, 1974; Meyer, 1975). Since the models represent concepts rather than individual words, paraphrases and synonym substitutions are permissible in recall. The models have not been widely adopted by experimenters, however, because of their complexity. A second type of model that can assist in scoring decisions is the "story grammar" (Mandler & Johnson, 1977; Rumelhart, 1975; Stein & Glenn, 1978; Thorndyke, 1977), which will be discussed in the final section of the chapter. This model, however, is applicable only to a limited class of prose materials: the story.

The major point we wish to communicate is that there is no way to get a complete, unbiased picture of what has been comprehended. However, by using a variety of test procedures, we can hope to obtain a reasonably accurate idea of what the reader has taken away from his or her interaction with a text.

When studying the *development* of comprehension, additional factors must be taken into consideration. For example, if we want to compare differences in comprehension skills among kindergarten, second, and fourth graders, it makes little sense to ask them to read a passage because the older children can read better than the younger. Thus, in order to avoid confounding differences in decoding ability with differences in comprehension, passages are often presented orally rather than in written form. Another way to avoid this problem is to present narratives in picture format rather than verbal; this approach has the added advantage of sustaining the child's interest level. While there is reason to believe that medium of presentation may affect comprehension (Schallert, Kleiman, & Rubin, 1977), this will not be a focus of our review.

A second problem specific to developmental research is that older children generally remember more information than younger. However, this does not necessarily mean that they comprehended the material better. A number of additional factors contribute to this improved performance on memory tasks, such as improved mnemonic or study strategies, and more familiarity with testing procedures and task demands. Thus, we should expect to find differences in the amount of information that is recalled by children of various ages; such an outcome is of little theoretical interest or practical value. What is of interest is whether or not manipulations of a particular variable have differential effects as a function of age. For example, it is not very informative to find that older children recalled more from a passage than younger; it is informative to know that the difference was greater when the passage was presented in a disorganized format than in an organized format. Such an outcome would indicate developmental differences in the ability to deal with disruptions in logical sequence.

Identifying Main Ideas

Reading comprehension tests abound with questions requiring identification of main ideas. The frequency with which such "main idea" exercises are given to beginning readers is evidence that this skill is regarded as an important component of reading comprehension. Experimental investigations of children's understanding of main ideas have used three general approaches. One approach simply tests for recall of a passage and examines the relative incidence of main ideas in the recall protocols (e.g., Binet & Henri, 1894; Christie & Schumacher, 1975; Korman, 1945, cited in Yendovitskayz, 1971). A second approach is to present children with a passage and ask them to classify the information as to its importance level (Brown & Smiley, 1977). The third approach is to ask children to describe the main idea of a passage in their own words (e.g., Danner, 1976; Mal'tseva, cited in Smirnov et al., 1971–1972; Otto, Barrett, & Koenke, 1969).

An early study using the recall approach was carried out by Binet and Henri (1894; excerpted translation in Thieman & Brewer, 1978). Children ranging in age from nine to twelve listened to short prose passages of varying lengths and then recalled them. Binet and Henri reported that important ideas were remembered better than less important ideas by children of all ages. In another early study (Korman, 1945, cited in Yendovitskayz, 1971), children of four, five, and six years listened to fairy tales and then recalled them. Again, ideas which were related to the theme of the story were more frequently recalled than those which were less related.

A problem common to both studies was that the criteria for deciding the relative importance of ideas were not well specified. The authors presumably used their intuitions to identify the important elements, and it is not clear how much agreement there would be if different opinions were obtained. A more recent study by Christie and Schumacher (1975) attempted to take this problem into account. The authors constructed a 420-word passage that could be divided into 30 "idea units." College students were asked to select the 15 ideas which were most relevant to the theme, and the 15 which were least relevant. The passage was presented on tape to kindergarten, second, and fifth graders who were later asked to recall it. Again, recall was better for ideas judged theme relevant than theme irrelevant.

Although these results suggest than even kindergarteners are able to differentiate the main ideas from the details of a fairly complex story, this conclusion is suspect. Inspection of the story reveals that the theme irrelevant ideas were not simply details; they were deliberately introduced into the story and were noticeably irrelevant (Brown & Smiley, 1977). Thus, even though the kindergarteners differentiated these two classes of information, there is no guarantee that they would be able to do so with "unrigged" stories.

Acknowledging the subjectivity of the previous assessments of importance, Brown and Smiley adopted a more systematic method for determining structural importance, developed by Johnson (1970). This method first requires that a passage be divided into units that correspond to points at which a speaker would pause. Next, raters are told that the units differ in terms of their importance to the passage and that some of the units can be eliminated without damaging the essence or "semantic cohesiveness" of the text. Units are then classified into four levels of structural importance by first eliminating one quarter of the units judged to be least important to the theme, then the quarter judged next least important, on up to the most important. Although this method lacks a strong theoretical rationale for either the initial parsing of the units or the subsequent ratings, it is a relatively simple way to operationalize importance. Furthermore, it yields a strong predictor of recall:

Johnson found that the higher a particular unit was rated in importance, the more likely its recall by college students.

Brown and Smiley used Johnson's method to determine whether children's recall patterns were also sensitive to the four levels of structural importance. The materials consisted of four non-Western fairy tales of about fifth grade reading level, chosen for their unfamiliarity to most American children. The fairy tales, parsed and rated by college students, were presented on tape to children in third, fifth, and seventh grades and were then recalled. The structural importance ratings were a strong predictor of recall: Important ideas were more likely to be recalled than less important ideas and all four levels of importance were different from one another in terms of amount recalled. Despite differences in total recall, this same pattern was obtained for children of all three ages as well as college students. Of most interest was the finding that children as young as eight years were sensitive to fairly subtle gradations in importance. However, six year olds were not able to differentiate the four levels of importance (Smiley et al., 1977). Although the most important ideas were best recalled, there were no real differences in recall of the three lower levels.

The studies discussed thus far suggest that young children recall more of the important information in a passage than the unimportant. However, they provide no indication that young children can deliberately *identify* the main ideas of a text. It is possible that differential recall occurs for reasons other than a deliberate attempt to attend to important ideas during reading or listening. For example, Brown and Smiley note that important ideas are usually actions, whereas ideas of lesser importance tend to be static descriptions. Thus, better recall may result from better memory for events and actions, rather than from explicit identification of the important elements. It has been shown, in fact, that actions are generally better recalled than static descriptions (e.g., Bartlett, 1932; Gomulicki, 1956).

In an effort to determine if children are consciously aware of the differences in relative importance of information contained within a passage, Brown and Smiley (1977) asked students in third, fifth, and seventh grades and college to perform the structural importance rating task. The classifications were then compared to the original ratings done by college students. Third graders were unsuccessful at differentiating levels; their ratings were idiosyncratic, with most units receiving the full range of scores. The fifth graders succeeded in separating the highest level from the other three, which were not differentiated. Seventh graders had somewhat better discrimination: Levels 1 and 2 were differentiated, as were levels 3 and 4, but levels 2 and 3 were not. Only the college students differentiated all four levels.

Although these results suggest that third graders are unable to identify even the most important elements in a passage, it should be noted that this rating task is rather difficult. A number of factors may have contributed to poor performance, among them the complexity of the material; the stories were approximately two years beyond third grade reading level. If the children were unable to comprehend parts of the text, we could hardly expect them to be able to rank the units for structural importance. (This complexity undoubtedly contributed to the low recall scores obtained by the third graders.) Furthermore, the units that the children were asked to rate were rather small, corresponding, for the most part, to phrases. It is possible that the children would be more successful at differentiating levels of importance if they dealt with larger meaning units, where the relationship of the part to the whole was more salient.

Bearing in mind that the children's performance would probably be better if the task were simplified, it is interesting to compare the recall results with the rating data. Brown and Smiley found that children from third grade up showed differential recall of the four importance levels, yet not even seventh graders were successful at classifying the units into four levels. One way to account for this discrepancy is to assume that young children's sensitivity to main ideas is below the level of awareness. In other words, selective attention to important elements may be a relatively automatic component of the comprehension process, while overt identification of these elements requires more conscious evaluation of the material. Brown and Smiley suggest this is a problem of "metacognition"; young children appear to have limited knowledge about their own cognitive processes (Brown, 1975b; Flavell & Wellman, 1977).

It should be obvious that the importance rating task is not the sort of task teachers would use if they wanted to find out if their students could identify main ideas. Although such a task would be useful in revealing whether students could construct a complete outline or efficiently select items for further study, it is too complex to be a good test of comprehension of main ideas. (And, indeed, Brown and Smiley did not intend it to be.)

A few experiments have used more straightforward methods of assessing main idea identification skills, but these studies have a number of weaknesses. In an early study, Mal'tseva (cited in Smirnov et al., 1971) asked children in grades two, four, and six to compose an outline of a narrative text, highlighting the most important information. The main ideas were extracted by 46 percent of the children in second grade, 58 percent in fourth, and 65 percent in sixth. With increasing age, then, children were better able to discriminate the important from the unimportant. Otto, Barrett, and Koenke (1969) had children identify the main idea in simple, four-sentence passages. Their instructions were to "make up just one sentence in your own words that says what all the sentences (in the passage) tell you." Only 29 percent of the second grade children were able to provide an adequate summary statement; most added a considerable amount of detail. In a similar experiment by Danner (1976), children from grades two, four, and six were asked to identify "the one thing that the sentences in the paragraph tell you about." All children correctly identified two-thirds of the main ideas, and 79 percent of them identified all. Although older children were more successful, even second graders performed well on this task.

These studies demonstrate that by the time children are in second grade, they have some skill in identifying main ideas. However, the children's abilities may actually be underestimated because of task variables. For example, the children may have been quite successful at extracting main ideas, but they had difficulty producing sentences that adequately expressed them.

Moreover, the children may not have understood the rather cryptic instructions they received in the Otto et al. study. Danner optimized his subjects' performance by giving them a number of orienting tasks, but it is not clear that sufficient practice was provided in the other experiments.

The research is also subject to a criticism raised earlier: There were no explicit criteria for determining the relative importance of ideas. The investigators presumably identified the main ideas themselves and scored the responses for consistency with their subjective standards. Although this is undoubtedly the approach taken by many teachers in evaluating their students' answers, it would nonetheless be desirable to have more objective criteria.

One additional factor to be considered in evaluating the main idea research is that there may be developmental differences in the conception of a main idea. Thus, although the responses did not conform to an adult standard, they may have been consistent with the conception of a main idea at a particular age. This suggestion has received support in a study by Stein and Glenn (1978). Children in first and fifth grades were asked to recall the three most important things that they remembered from a story. The ratings were collected in a successive manner by asking for the first most important thing in the story, the second, then the third. Age differences were obtained in the types of information considered most important. First graders generally focused on the consequences of actions, while fifth graders focused more on the goals of characters in the story. These results suggest that first graders do have consistent ideas as to what is most important in a story; their ideas just differ from older children's ideas. What remains to be determined is the reason for developmental shift in importance judgments. One possibility is that the meaning of importance undergoes changes. For example, older children may regard information as important because it helps them organize and remember a text, whereas younger children may consider information important because of its moral value. This is a highly speculative possibility; it is clear that a more thorough investigation of the conception of importance is needed.

In summary, it appears that children as young as five years of age are sensitive to main ideas to the extent that they are more likely to recall main ideas than details. However, it is not clear that this differential recall arises from a deliberate increase in attention to the important elements of the text. This is substantiated by the apparent difficulty young children have in explicitly distinguishing important from unimportant information and their less than perfect attempts to summarize main ideas.

Understanding Logical Structure

In addition to extracting main ideas from a passage, an important element of comprehension is understanding how and why the ideas are interconnected. Skill at understanding the logical structure of a text is firmly rooted in prior knowledge of the world. For example, if children do not understand how two events in the physical world are logically related, we can hardly expect them to perceive this relationship in a text. It should be noted that some of the studies to be reviewed in this section are not explicitly focused on prose comprehension, but rather the comprehension of logical and temporal relations. They are presented here because they deal with what we believe is an important prerequisite of prose understanding.

Piaget (1926) is responsible for much of the recent interest in sensitivity to logical structure. He reported that in retelling stories, young children frequently mixed up the order of events and expressed causal connections poorly or not at all. He attributed these problems to the child's inability to make use of logical relations. However, the stories Piaget used were lengthy and complex, and so perhaps were difficult to comprehend.

In an effort to clarify Piaget's claims, Brown carried out an extensive program of research investigating children's comprehension and memory for ordered sequences of events. (See Brown, 1976a, for a complete review.) In one set of experiments, Brown and Murphy (1975) presented four year old children with sets of pictures that depicted either a logical sequence of events or an arbitrary sequence. The logical pictures were arranged in either normal or scrambled order. After presentation, the children were asked to reconstruct the ordering of the pictures in each set. Reconstruction was better on ordered logical sequences than on arbitrary or scrambled sequences. This indicates that the children understood the logical structure of the pictures and were able to use their prior knowledge about logical relations to improve memory. Another experiment demonstrated that the same set of unrelated pictures was better reconstructed when it was accompanied by a narrative which meaningfully interrelated the pictures. Since the pictures themselves were unrelated, the results cannot simply be attributed to correct construction of the order on the basis of prior knowledge alone.

In a similar study, Brown (1975a) tested the hypothesis that the recall failures reported by Piaget were due to excessive memory demands rather than comprehension difficulties. Kindergarten and second graders were shown sets of pictures accompanied by a logically structured or an arbitrarily sequenced narrative. In a third condition, children were instructed to make up their own story to help remember the pictures. After viewing the pictures, the children were asked to recognize, reconstruct, or recall the sequences. As before, performance was worse when the narratives were arbitrarily ordered than when they were logically connected. Moreover, the sequences which went with the self-constructed stories were as well-remembered as the logically-structured sequences. Second graders performed equally well on all memory tasks, but for kindergarteners, recognition was better than reconstruction which was in turn better than recall. Thus, the more external cues available, the better the performance. This study supports a point made earlier: Recall difficulties do not necessarily reflect failures to comprehend.

Brown's experiments demonstrate quite convincingly that children as young as four years of age understand logical relationships expressed either verbally or pictorially. Moreover, the children are capable of capitalizing on these logical relationships to enhance memory of the material. Thus, we have evidence that beginning readers possess the prerequisite skills necessary for comprehending logical structure in prose. It has been shown, in fact, that five year olds are very accurate in recalling the order of events in short stories that are logically organized (Mandler & Johnson, 1977; Stein & Glenn, 1978).

It appears, however, that young children's comprehension is impaired when the presented order of events does not conform to a logical sequence. For example, French and Brown (1976) and Homzie and Gravitt (1976) found that preschoolers had poorer comprehension of sentences in which the order of mention was different from the order of occurrence (i.e., "Before Raggedy Ann calls the doctor, the dog bites the baby"). The disruption was less detrimental when the events were logically rather than arbitrarily related, indicating that the children perceived and benefitted from the logical structure. That young children have difficulty dealing with inverted sequences is not necessarily an indication that they are deficient in a critical comprehension skill. Adults, too, exhibit poorer memory of inverted than forward-order sequences (Baker, 1978; Clark & Clark, 1968).

Nevertheless, there appear to be developmental differences in children's ability to deal with disruptions in logical structure. This is reflected primarily in the strategies children use to impose a meaningful organization on the material. For example, Poulson, Kintsch, Kintsch, and Premack (in press) presented four and six year old children with sets of 15 to 18 pictures that depicted a story. A nonmemory method of assessing comprehension was used: Children were asked to describe the pictures one by one as they studied them (after having already viewed the complete set), and their descriptions were compared with adults' descriptions. The pictures were presented in either correct logical order or scrambled, in which case it was extremely difficult for children to perceive the correct sequence.

Most of the descriptions children produced were responses to some feature of the stimulus picture, but they also made responses that could only be derived through an understanding of the story. Twice as many such "story propositions" were produced when the story was intact, which is to be expected since the scrambled pictures did not depict an obvious story. However, many *inappropriate* story propositions were added in the descriptions of the scrambled stories, indicating that the children were trying to impose a logical structure on the picture set. Six year olds did this more frequently than four year olds, and they used more inappropriate story propositions when the story was scrambled than they used appropriate propositions when it was intact. Apparently, when the story was well-structured, the children felt it would be redundant to add story propositions, but when it was scrambled, additions were needed in order to make the logical structure more apparent. Thus, the six year olds seemed to be making up a story as they described the scrambled pictures. In contrast, the younger children frequently reverted to a strategy of labeling the pictures.

Stein (1976) also demonstrated developmental differences in the strategies children use to deal with disruptions in logical structure. In addition, her experiment was a more sensitive test of children's understanding of logical relations among events, in that she used prose stories with subtle disruptions in logical order rather than picture stories with extreme disruptions. Starting with three logically ordered stories, she systematically distorted them by moving specific statements away from their points of origin. (These statements correspond to "categories" in story-grammar terminology. Further details will be provided later in the chapter.) In one case, the statement was simply inverted with its neighbor, while in the other conditions, it was separated by more statements. Subjects in second and sixth grades listened to the stories and then recalled them.

Although sixth graders recalled more information than second graders, the general patterns of recall were similar. In general, the distorted stories were more poorly recalled than the well-formed stories, with greater effects the further the movement from the original position. Of most interest were the types of reorganizational strategies children used when they encountered a disruption. If the statement was simply inverted, subjects tended to switch it back to its logical position. With larger movements, children often repeated the statement; it was mentioned in the position in which it was heard, but it was also mentioned in the position it should appear. Thus, children remembered the position of the displacement, but they repeated the statement and sometimes added new information to make the story conform to a better structure. The older children were more successful than the younger in reconciling the discrepancies.

In Stein's experiment (1976), the stories were illogical when they were temporally disorganized; there was nothing to alert the reader that the events had been mentioned out of their proper story sequence. It is possible that if the inversions were marked in the text, there would be fewer disruptions in recall. This was confirmed in an experiment by Stein and Nezworski (1977); similar types of inversions were used, but markers such as "This happened because . . ." were included as signals that the order of mention deviated from the order of occurrence. For fifth graders, marked inversions were at least as well recalled as when the information appeared in correct order, and some inversions were actually better recalled. For first graders, some inversions were recalled as in well-formed stories, but some were worse. This indicates that young children's comprehension is more dependent upon consistence with a forward-order logical sequence than that of the older children. First graders are probably less familiar with temporal inversions as a stylistic device in stories and so are less able to deal with them.

Similar conclusions were drawn by Mandler (1978). She constructed four two-episode stories, and then violated the logical sequence by interleaving statements from the two episodes. Each story began with a common setting, followed by alternating statements from each episode. Subjects in second, fourth, and sixth grades, as well as college students, listened to either normal or interleaved stories on tape and recalled them 24 hours later. Not surprisingly, standard stories were better recalled than interleaved. In recalling interleaved stories, subjects frequently repeated the statements in their logical position of mention, a strategy similar to that observed by Stein (1976). Children of all ages were more likely to recall the interleaved stories in their logical sequence than were adults; they tended to separate the stories into discrete episodes, whereas the adults recalled the stories in their order of presentation. Mandler attributes this re-organization to a lack of familiarity with discrepant structures; in order to remember a story, children need to make it conform to a logical sequence.

These studies have shown that children are sensitive to logical structure in stories, since deviations lead to decrements in recall. Furthermore, it is clear that children begin to develop strategies for dealing with the deviations by the time they are in first or second grade, as evidenced by their attempts to reconstruct a logical sequence. Thus, these studies are further evidence that skill at understanding how and why ideas are interconnected within a story develops very early, probably before the child has begun to read.

Up to this point, our discussion has focused on children's sensitivity to logical structure in picture and oral narratives. Awareness of logical structure in expository prose is also an important concern, but few studies deal with this type of text. Danner (1976), however, has carried out an initial investigation. He constructed two short passages containing four topics related to an overall theme. In the organized versions, each paragraph dealt with one topic, while in the disorganized versions, each paragraph contained sentences about different topics. Children in grades two, four, and six listened to the taped passages and subsequently recalled them, with each subject hearing an organized version of one passage and a disorganized version of the second. The amount of text recalled was greater for the organized than the unorganized versions, and older children recalled more than younger children. In the organized versions, all children tended to group together those ideas that were related to a particular topic sentence; however, developmental differences in grouping strategies were observed with unorganized texts. Older children reorganized the statements to conform to the logical, topical grouping, whereas younger children did not.

After the recall task, the children were tested for their understanding of logical organization: They were asked which passage was more difficult and why; they were asked to state the differences between the organized and disorganized passages; and they were asked to group a random arrangement of sentences into their topical groupings. On all tasks, older children performed better than younger children, suggesting differences in the awareness of the organization that can be built into text material. For example, all children reported that the disorganized passages were more difficult, but only the older children could show the experimenter how the two passages differed or could actually state that one passage was "mixed up" and the other in "the correct order." Furthermore, older children could more easily group sentences in a passage around specific topic sentences.

Danner's results show an interesting parallel with Brown and Smiley's 1977 findings. Whereas all children appeared to be sensitive to discrepancies in logical structure as reflected by amount recalled, only the older children were able to explain why the passages differed in difficulty. Again, we see evidence of a metacognitive deficit. The results also invite the speculation that children develop an understanding of logical structure in expository prose at a later age than they do in stories. This could result because children are exposed to narratives from the time they first begin to understand language, while experience with expository text is infrequent before third grade.

In conclusion, comprehension of logical structure is an early-developing skill. Children's knowledge about logical relationships and structure greatly influences their memory for prose material. Those passages that are organized according to an underlying logical structure are better remembered than arbitrarily sequenced or disorganized passages. The studies reviewed, however, illustrated that there are developmental differences in the skills brought to these tasks. These differences seem to be related to children's awareness that logical structure has a facilitative effect on memory. Older children were more flexible and competent in using active strategies to increase memory for disorganized material. An important area of future investigation is the process by which this flexibility and awareness of logical structure develops.

Making Inferences

In order to understand the main ideas of a text and perceive their interrelationships, it is often necessary to bring in information that is not explicitly presented in the text. Many of the things readers need to know to comprehend prose are not explicitly stated; therefore, they must be able to draw upon prior knowledge of the world to make inferences and fill in "gaps" in the flow of ideas. That comprehension involves an interaction between the incoming information and what a person already knows has been persuasively argued by Bartlett (1932). By providing numerous examples of prose recall protocols, he demonstrated that meaning is not inherent in a text but must be constructed by the reader and so may differ depending on experience, attitudes, and context.

Bartlett's ideas have been influential in stimulating research on the role of inferences in prose comprehension. Although most of the studies have used adult subjects (see Bransford & McCarrell, 1974), developmental psychologists have also become interested in the problem. Much of this work has been reviewed thoroughly elsewhere (Paris, 1975; Paris & Lindauer, 1977; Tarbasso & Nicholas, 1977), so our discussion will be relatively brief.

We would like to note at the outset that the research on children's inferencing skills leaves much to be desired. In many studies, it is not clear that the children's performance can even be attributed to the use of inferences. Moreover, the most commonly used experimental task is far removed from normal reading situations. Nevertheless, the work deserves mention, if only to show how many questions are still unanswered.

One of the most frequently tested hypotheses emerging from Bartlett's work (1932) is that people construct an integrated semantic representation as they read or listen to prose and that as a result of this integration, it is sometimes difficult to distinguish the actual text content from inferred information. This hypothesis was tested developmentally by Paris & Carter (1973), after it received support in an adult study by Bransford, Barclay, and Franks (1972). The materials in both experiments consisted of sets of three related sentences, two premises and one filler. An example is:

> The bird is in the cage.   (premise)
> The cage is under the table.   (premise)
> The bird is yellow.   (filler)

The two premise sentences allow one to infer the transitive relationship, "The bird is under the table." Of critical interest is the extent to which subjects falsely indicate that this true inference had been a member of the acquisition set. In addition to the true inference, recognition items included a true premise ("The bird is in the cage"); a false premise ("The cage is over the table"); and a false inference ("The bird is on top of the table").

In the Paris and Carter study, seven sets of sentences were read aloud to children in second and fifth grades. After a five minute delay, the children were given the recognition statements and were asked to decide if they were exactly the same as those studied. Although second graders made more errors than fifth graders, their response patterns were similar. Children in both grades consistently made errors on true inferences; in fact, they were as likely to identify true inferences as "old" as they were to label true premises "old." The children were considerably more accurate in labeling both false premises and false inferences as "new."

These data led Paris and Carter to conclude that children, like adults, construct the semantic relationships among ideas and integrate them in the representation stored in memory; this creates difficulty discriminating inferred from explicit information. Brown (1976b) and Paris and Mahoney (1974) reported similar results using pictorial materials. In all studies, the fact that even the youngest children had difficulty recognizing true inferences as "new" was taken as evidence that the ability to make inferences develops relatively early.

However, a number of factors cast doubt on the conclusion that the children were in fact drawing inferences. For example, Trabasso and Nicholas (1977) suggest that the children may have had a loose decision criterion; that is, they said "old" whenever a statement was semantically consistent, even if it could be discriminated from an actual premise. A second problem arises from the fact that the false statements on the recognition task introduced new relational terms while the true statements retained the original terms (Trabasso & Nicholas, 1977; Thieman & Brown,1977). Thus, it is possible that children falsely recognized true inferences as "old" items because the relational term was the same and not because they had made the appropriate inference. Some support for this alternative explanation has been provided by Thieman and Brown. Finally, young children are notorious for their bias to respond "old" to items on recognition tests. This bias is particularly a problem when the data of primary interest are incorrect "old" responses.

A recent study by Kail et al. (1977) provides somewhat better evidence that children can and do make inferences. The earlier paradigm was modified by having children decide if the test sentences were consistent with, rather than identical to, the stories. This modification eliminated reliance on false recognition errors as an index of inferencing, since responses are *correct* if true inferences are classified as semantically consistent. Materials were similar to those used by Paris and Carter (1973), except that some of the three sentence stories allowed contextual, rather than transitive, inferences. For example, "Mary was playing in a game. She was hit by a bat," invites the inference, "Mary was playing baseball." Children in second and sixth grades read the sentences aloud from slides, controlling presentation times themselves. After the presentation of each story, subjects received one premise and one inference question.

Children at both grade levels showed greater than chance accuracy on all types of questions, and second graders were comparable to fourth. Of most interest was the fact that subjects frequently judged true inferences to be semantically consistent, while correctly judging false statements inconsistent. Thus, this study strengthens the earlier claim that even the younger children made inferences. Furthermore, it shows that they have the ability to make "gap-filling" inferences, i.e., supplying the omitted information that the game was baseball, as well as the "text-connecting" inferences that establish intersentence relationships. It is much harder to argue that the contextual inferences were simply an artifact of the testing procedure.

In all of the studies discussed thus far, the investigators concluded that the inferences were made during initial exposure to the story and stored in memory along with the explicit information. However, it is possible that inferences were not made until the time of test, prompted by the recognition statements. Thus, the data do not indicate that children made inferences during reading but simply that they can make inferences. Of course, knowing that children can make inferences at all is really of most importance. Besides, children should not be encouraged to make *all* possible inferences as they read, but only those which are necessary. It is not clear that they *must* make the transitive inference, "The bird is under the table," in order to understand "The bird is in the cage. The cage is under the table."

In view of the limitations of his earlier work, Paris (Paris & Upton, 1976) provided a more sensitive test of children's ability to draw inferences from prose. The materials consisted of passages that were seven or eight sentences in length, as opposed to the simple sentence or picture sets used previously. The passages described behaviors and incidents familiar to young children (e.g., raiding the cookie jar). Eight yes/no probe questions were constructed for each passage, half of which required inferences and half tested memory for verbatim information. The required inferences were of two basic types: those that could be made from single lexical items (e.g., inferring that scissors were used to *cut* some paper), and those that depended on contextual relations within and between sentences (e.g., inferring that a child who tried to help a wounded bird liked to take care of animals).

Subjects were children in grades K–5, who listened to each story as it was read aloud and then answered the eight questions. The older children made more correct responses than younger children on both verbatim and inferential questions, but the difference was greater on inferences. Further analysis of the data revealed that the developmental improvement in making contextual inferences was not simply due to better memory of the stories (although the lexical inference improvement was). This result led Paris and Upton to conclude that children's inference-making skills do improve with age, contrary to Paris' earlier conclusion (Paris & Carter, 1973).

A second experiment by Paris and Upton (1976) examined the relationship of performance on the probe task to a subsequent test of free recall. Recall accuracy correlated highly with the ability to draw contextual inferences at each grade level, and this correlation increased with age. The authors concluded that inferencing enhances recall and that the older the child, the more recall is improved. Although this conclusion is intriguing, it should be regarded as tentative: The correlation does not indicate that inferencing *caused* improved recall but simply that the two were somehow related.

A few recent studies have provided perhaps the most unambiguous evidence that young children can draw inferences from prose material. These studies have all used a questioning technique specifically designed to elicit inferences. Brown, Smiley, Day, Townsend, and Lawton (1977) presented children in second, fourth, and sixth grades with passages that could be interpreted with respect to a previously provided framework. A series of probe questions indicated that the children had accessed information from the orienting framework to aid in the comprehension of the story. (See Levin, this volume, for a more thorough discussion of the study.) Stein and Glenn (1978) and Omanson, Warren, and Trabasso (1978) also found that young children could draw inferences from stories. Although the inferences were not always those an older child or adult would have made, it was clear that the children accessed their previous knowledge in dealing with the new material.

In summary, despite weaknesses in many of the experiments we reviewed, the available evidence is sufficiently compelling to conclude that children can and do make inferences about prose material, calling upon their general knowledge of the world to supplement explicit information. Several issues remain to be clarified, however, such as children's awareness of the inference process, the conditions under which inferences are made, and whether or not inferences influence memory.

Using Higher Order Knowledge Structures

Throughout this chapter, we have argued that comprehension involves an interaction between the reader's background knowledge and the text itself. Prior knowledge plays a crucial role in all of the skills we have discussed: extracting main ideas, understanding logical structure, and drawing inferences. When using these skills, specific knowledge may be brought to bear on particular segments of text; for example, we access our knowledge about tools that can be used for cutting paper to infer that "scissor" was the implied instrument in the sentence "She cut the paper." Situations also arise where more generic knowledge can be used to enhance comprehension. For example, people have generalized knowledge about stories, with specific expectations about their structural components. Similarly, people often have general knowledge about the structure of reading materials specific to their field, i.e., journal articles. Such organized collections of knowledge are known as "higher order" knowledge structures or "schemata." Schemata are thought to facilitate comprehension because they can be used as an organizing framework within which to integrate incoming information. (See Anderson, 1977 and Rumelhart & Ortony, 1977, for further discussion of the role of schemata in comprehension.)

Within the past few years, several investigators have attempted to describe the higher order of structures that are used to encode, represent, and retrieve information in stories. Attention has focused on the story because of the regularity in its underlying logical structure. That is, despite variations in content, linguists have observed a stable organizational pattern governing the types of information and logical relations that exist in most stories (Colby & Cole, 1973; Levi-Strauss, 1955; Prince, 1973; Propp, 1958). Whereas linguists have been concerned primarily with the structure of the stories *per se*, psychologists have been more interested in the knowledge people have about the structure of stories. This knowledge has been described in a number of different grammars for stories (Mandler & Johnson, 1977; Rumelhart, 1975; Stein & Glenn, 1978; Thorndyke, 1977). Despite some differences in terminology and degree of elaboration, the major characteristics of the grammars are similar. The Stein and Glenn grammar will be summarized here for illustrative purposes.

Table 1 provides an example of a simple story that has been partitioned into categories, the basic units of analysis in the Stein and Glenn grammar. The story is considered well-formed because it contains all of the requisite categories, arranged in their correct logical sequence. A simple story can first be broken down into two parts: a setting category plus an episode structure. The *setting* begins the story with the introduction of a protagonist and normally includes information about the social, physical, or temporal context of the story. The episode is the primary higher order unit of analysis and consists of five categories of information. These categories serve particular functions in the story and occur in fixed temporal sequence. The *initiating event* category contains an event or action that changes the story environment. The major function of this change is to evoke the formation of a goal. The goal is included in the *internal response* category. Internal responses also include affective states and cognitions, and they serve to motivate a character's subsequent overt behavior. Overt actions that are directed towards goal attainment are classified as *attempts*. The result of an attempt is the *consequence*, which marks the attainment or nonattainment of a goal. The final category is the *reaction*, which can include either a character's response to the consequence or broader consequences of the goal attainment.

Table 1
Category Breakdown of a Well-formed Story

Setting	1. Once there was a big grey fish named Albert
	2. who lived in a big icy pond near the edge of a forest
Initiating Event	3. One day, Albert was swimming around the pond
	4. when he spotted a big juicy worm on top of the water
Internal Response	5. Albert knew how delicious worms tasted
	6. and wanted to eat that one for his dinner
Attempt	7. So he swam very close to the worm
	8. and bit into him
Consequence	9. Suddenly, Albert was pulled through the water into a boat
	10. He had been caught by a fisherman
Reaction	11. Albert felt sad
	12. and wished he had been more careful

In reality, few stories have a structure as simple as the one described; most stories contain many episodes, and these may be connected by various types of logical relations. Similarly, stories may also contain incomplete episodes, where one or more of the basic categories is omitted. In such cases, it is assumed that the reader infers the information contained in the missing category. However, if too many categories are missing, and/or the logical connections are vague, people will not be able to construct an adequate representation of the story. Such stories are not considered "well-formed."

This brief description of a story grammar is admittedly over-simplified due to space limitations. The main point we want to convey is that there are rules governing the kinds of information that should appear in a story and the order in which this information appears.

A number of recent experiments have tested predictions about story comprehension and memory based on the grammars (Glenn, 1978; Mandler, 1978; Mandler & Johnson, 1977; Rumelhart, 1975; Stein, 1976; Stein & Glenn, 1977a, b, 1978; Stein & Nezworski, 1978; Thorndyke, 1977). This work is discussed in detail in Stein (in press) and the interested reader is referred to that source. One of the major conclusions that has emerged is that knowledge of the structure of stories is critical to an understanding of stories. Therefore, it is important to study the development of this knowledge and its role in children's comprehension.

A straightforward way to assess children's knowledge of story structure is to ask them to produce a story. If they do have knowledge about the kinds of information that belong in stories, then this information should appear in their constructions. Stein and Glenn (1977a) provided kindergartners and third and fifth graders with story settings and asked them to finish the stories. The children's stories were classified according to their structure, which ranged from simple descriptions through complex episodes. The more sophisticated structures were characterized by their inclusion of purposive behaviors and increasingly well-specified motives and goals. Only about half of the kindergartners' stories contained purposive behaviors, while two thirds of the third graders' stories were purposive, as were almost all of the fifth graders'. Thus, there was a clear developmental progression in the logical complexity of the stories, presumably reflecting increasing knowledge of the constituents of a well-formed story.

Leondar (1977) also found a strong relationship between age and the structural complexity of stories produced by children ranging in age from three to sixteen. Similarly, Sutton-Smith and his colleagues (Botvin & Sutton-Smith, 1977; Sutton-Smith, Botvin, & Mahoney, 1976) reported high correlations between age and several hypothesized levels of structural complexity in the stories constructed by children from three to twelve years of age. Although all of the investigators used different indices of structural complexity, they observed strikingly similar developmental patterns. Perhaps of most importance is the common observation that children as young as four and five years of age were capable of constructing well-formed, purposive stories. This finding conflicts with Piaget's 1926 claim that children lack the cognitive structures to produce a coherent story before the age of seven or eight. All of these experiments suggest that children acquire knowledge about story structure at a very early age and use it to guide their story construction.

The extent to which such knowledge influences comprehension and memory of stories has also been investigated. The basic paradigm is to present children with short stories and ask for recall. The primary focus is on qualitative aspects of recall, rather than quantitative; in other words, researchers are more concerned with the kinds of information children remember from stories than the overall amount. Stein and Glenn (1978) presented first and fifth graders with children's stories that had been analyzed according to their grammar. The older children recalled more than the younger, but recall of specific statements was stable over grades. Some categories were more salient than others, as indicated by their frequency of recall. Major settings were best recalled, closely followed by initiating events and consequences. Internal responses were poorly recalled, except when they contained goal statements. The only consistent developmental difference was that fifth graders recalled more internal responses than first graders. This parallels the increasing emphasis on motivations reflected in children's story construction and importance ratings (Stein & Glenn, 1978). [We should point out that this trend is not specific to stories, but appears in children's understanding of many types of social interactions (Flappan, 1968)].

Stein and Glenn (1978) also examined information that had not been contained in the original stories but was introduced in recall. More intrusions were made by fifth graders than first, and the intrusions frequently belonged to the internal responses and attempt categories. The fact that internal responses were poorly recalled would lead one to believe that children are insensitive to psychological states of the characters; however, the high proportion of internal response intrusions indicates that this is not so. In fact, a second experiment by Stein and Glenn (1978) directly probed children's perceptions of causality in the stories, and showed that all children regarded a character's intentions and motivations as the primary cause of the consequence. Responses to a series of "why" questions revealed that even the first graders had good comprehension of the logical relationships existing among the story categories.

Mandler and Johnson (1977) also examined qualitative aspects of story recall using four short stories analyzed according to their grammar (Stein and Glenn's terminology will be used here since it has already been introduced). Children in the first and fourth grades, and college adults, listened to and recalled the stories. Adults recalled more information than fourth graders, who in turn recalled more than first. Age differences were observed in the amount recalled from specific categories, but the patterning of recall was similar. Settings were best recalled by the first graders, closely followed by initiating events and then consequences. Recall was progressively worse for attempts, reactions, and internal responses. Fourth graders had the same ordering of category recall except that attempts were as well recalled as consequences. Adults recalled attempts, settings, initiating events, and consequences equally well, but reactions and internal responses were still significantly worse. These commonalities suggest that young children are sensitive to the same structural components in stories as adults. The results are consistent with those of Stein and Glenn (1978) in showing differential recall of specific categories. It appears that story grammar analyses can predict what information will be remembered on the basis of its structural role in the story.

A major prediction derived from story grammar analyses is that stories which conform to the prototypical structure will be better remembered than those that do not. Stein and Glenn (1977b) tested this hypothesis by examining the effects of category deletions on children's story recall. They constructed four stories that contained all six categories specified by their grammar and created five variations by deleting one category from the episode. Children in first and fifth grades listened to and recalled either well-formed stories or their structural variants. Fifth graders recalled more than first, but in general, the category deletions did not have the anticipated disruptive effects on recall. However, for both grades, recall was disrupted when the initiating event of the story was deleted, and first graders showed decreased recall when the consequence was deleted.

An analysis of the intrusions in recall proved informative. Fifth graders made more inferences than first graders except when the stories were well formed or when the reaction was deleted. There were more inferences relative to the well-formed story when the initiating event, attempt or consequence was deleted, but no increases with deletions of the internal response or reaction. It is interesting to note that it is when the most frequently recalled categories (initiating events and consequences) are deleted that most new information is added to recall. Similarly, the deletions of these categories produced the largest decrement in accurate recall. The added information was often of the same category type as that which was deleted; that is, if an initiating event was deleted, children would infer one; if a consequence was deleted, a new one would be inferred. This study provides further evidence that young children do have knowledge of story structure and that they use that knowledge to make deviant stories conform to the norm. Nevertheless, developmental differences were apparent in the skill with which gap-filling inferences could be made.

A related prediction of story grammars is that comprehension and/or memory will be impaired if the presentation of a story violates the prototypical sequence of categories. Since a disruption in category sequence produces a disruption in the logical flow of ideas, it is intuitively clear that this prediction would be supported by empirical test. In fact, we have already described the studies which have been undertaken as specific tests of this hypothesis in the section on logical structure (Mandler, 1978; Stein, 1976; Stein & Nezworski, 1977). To reiterate, these studies demonstrated that young children are sensitive to disruptions in story sequence, as reflected by decrements in recall and attempts to reorganize the story to conform to a more logical structure.

In summary, it appears that knowledge about the structure of stories develops during the preschool years. Most children's exposure to stories begins before they can even talk, so it is not surprising that a story schema is acquired quite early. The schema goes through refinement during the elementary school years, with an increasing focus on internal goals and responses. Several studies have provided evidence that children, as well as adults, benefit from the organizing framework of the story schema. Story grammars have been constructed to describe the schema and are useful as an approach toward understanding the comprehension process. The grammars offer a model of the strategies people might use when reading or listening to a story, enabling them to encode information efficiently.

Conclusions

What Can Researchers Tell Educators That They Don't Already Know?

As we cautioned at the beginning of the chapter, the relevance of many of these experiments to comprehension instruction is far from obvious; nevertheless, we claimed they were of practical significance. We will now defend this claim, but at the same time point out the limitations of the research and directions for further study.

It is undoubtedly true that many of the experiments we reviewed simply confirmed what reading teachers have always known: under the right conditions, young elementary school children can identify main ideas, understand logical structure, make inferences, and use knowledge about the structure of stories. Perhaps teachers would feel gratified to know that their intuitions and classroom observations have been supported experimentally, but they would probably prefer to be told something new. Since the new information provided by these experiments lies primarily in their implications, it will be helpful to make these implications explicit.

Of the skills we discussed, the one most directly relevant to comprehension instruction is main idea identification. The experiments showed that regardless of age, children have better memory for important than unimportant information in a passage. As we noted, however, recall does not necessarily reflect an ability to identify main ideas. The best way to find out if children can identify main ideas is to ask them directly, ideally with the text available to minimize memory demands. Although Brown and Smiley's importance ratings (1977) were obtained in such a way, the task complexity undoubtedly led to a low estimate of children's abilities. Using a much simpler task, Danner (1976) found that second graders could identify main ideas with some success. However, the passages he used were so short and simple that the older children may have found them insultingly easy. (This problem can arise whenever there is a large age range among subjects; materials that are the right level of complexity for one age group may not be appropriate for another.) Thus, we do not have much data on older children's main idea identification skills with more challenging passages. Moreover we do not know how skill at identifying main ideas changes with age.

We do know that there are developmental differences in the types of information children judge to be most important in stories (Stein & Glenn, 1978). There are undoubtedly individual and cultural differences as well, since everyone comes to the reading situation with different background experiences. However, the nature of the educational process requires that such differences be ironed out, for students are expected to extract the main ideas from their textbooks. Just how children learn to identify this normatively important information remains to be investigated.

The research on children's understanding of logical structure has fewer direct parallels in educational practice than the main idea research. Although children in the early grades are often asked to unscramble pictures or sentences to create a logical story, it is not until the upper grades that attention is devoted to teaching how and why ideas within a passage are interconnected.

One reason for this lack of early instruction may be that teachers feel children already understand logical relationships by the time they start to read. The research we reviewed demonstrates that preschoolers are, in fact, sensitive to logical structure in oral and picture narratives. The primary developmental difference in understanding logical structure seems to be in the strategies that are available for dealing with disorganized passages (Poulson et al., in press; Stein, 1976; Stein & Nezworski, 1977; Mandler, 1978). Although we don't really know how these strategies develop, experience alone must be an important factor.

In view of the increasingly dominant role of expository texts in the child's educational experience, further research on understanding expository text organization is needed. Although Danner's contribution is important, additional studies should extend his work using more complex materials. Such research would be valuable not only for comprehension instruction, but also for instruction in writing; children must understand logical organization in order to write logically organized prose.

The research we reviewed on inferences provides us with little more than the conclusion that children can draw inferences when asked questions about sentence triplets and simple stories. The extent to which children *spontaneously* draw inferences remains an empirical question, although there is some evidence that children will infer information that is crucial to comprehension (Brown et al., 1977; Stein & Glenn, 1978).

Given the methodological problems inherent in the inference research, the following generalizations should be regarded as tentative. There seems to be no evidence of developmental change in children's abilities to make inferences from sentence or picture triplets (Paris & Carter, 1973; Paris & Mahoney, 1974;

Kail et al., 1977). However, there were developmental differences in making inferences from stories. Paris and Upton (1976) reported that older children were better at making contextual inferences than younger, and Stein and Glenn (1978) reported age differences in children's ability to infer missing elements in a story. These discrepant findings may result from differences in the scope of the required inferences. That is, inferences based on the sentence sets could be made by considering two simple sentences, whereas with stories, inferences often dealt with the theme of the story as a whole. Thus, younger children may have had difficulty considering the many components of a story simultaneously; this conclusion is supported by the fact that when the inferences dealt with specific words and phrases from a story, the developmental differences were eliminated (Brown et al., 1977; Paris & Upton, 1976).

An important comprehension skill that we did not touch upon in our review of the literature, but which is related to inferencing, is the ability to consider new material in light of what is already known. Little or no research has focused on this higher level aspect of comprehension (which some do not consider to be comprehension *per se* but, rather, applying the products of comprehension) primarily because appropriate questions are difficult to formulate and are rather subjective. Nevertheless, this skill is crucial in answering "application" and "integration" questions frequently encountered on tests. Since even college students have difficulty with such questions, it is unlikely that young children consider incoming information with regard to a broader context of experience. By focusing too much on typical memory tests of learning and comprehension, such as free recall and recognition, educators run the risk of restricting students' intellectual creativity. Every teacher, for example, has probably encountered students who knew their course material by heart but failed a test because they were required to do some creative, integrative thinking. (See Baker & Santa, 1977 and Baker, Santa, & Gentry, 1977, for empirical demonstrations of this phenomenon.) Though the necessity for such "transsituational" comprehension increases as children become more involved in studying for content courses, it is probably never too early to introduce training in this skill.

The research dealing with children's understanding of story structure showed that children do in fact know what kinds of information belong in stories. Even four and five year olds are capable of constructing well-formed stories that include purposive behavior. The research shows that young children have excellent comprehension of stories that conform to the structure specified by the schema. However, their comprehension is impaired when stories deviate from the schema, and this impairment is greater than that which occurs for older children and adults. One source of this developmental difference is less familiarity with discrepant structures. Clearly, repeated experience with such stories allows one to build up strategies for dealing with them.

An important practical application of this research is to use the story grammar as a model for construction of instructional materials. Many of the materials currently prepared for beginning readers are sometimes little more than strings of sentences, lacking the conflicts and goals that are such crucial elements of stories (Bruce, 1978). It's no wonder, then, that many children regard reading as a boring task and not worth the effort. However, if stories were to conform to a story schema, not only would the children find them more comprehensible, but hopefully they would discover that reading can be intrinsically rewarding.

While it is important for beginning readers to enjoy reading, it is also important that they learn to read expository prose, a task that is usually not nearly as much fun as reading a good story. Virtually all of the experiments on prose comprehension development have used stories as stimulus materials. One reason for this focus is to maintain children's interest in the task, but the primary advantage of using stories is that their structures can be specified by story grammar analysis. Nevertheless, researchers must also investigate expository comprehension, particularly in children of the "transitional" period; i.e., third and fourth graders who have mastered basic decoding skills but are not yet fluent readers. It is often at this time that reading problems become apparent, both because of the shift in emphasis from decoding to comprehension and because the children are expected to deal with expository prose in their social studies and science books for the first time.

Although there are undoubtedly many commonalities underlying comprehension of stories and expositions, there are also many differences which should be explored. We know that children understand stories quite well at an early age, yet we do not know how well they understand expository prose. It is possible we would find something akin to what Piaget (1952) has termed a "horizontal décalage": a particular child may be quite capable of performing a certain mental operation (i.e., making an inference) with a story but not with an expository text. Similarly, as we suggested earlier, children may understand logical structure in narrative before expository text. A number of factors may contribute to this hypothesized décalage, the most obvious of which is the child's greater experience with stories. In addition, stories have a higher order structure specified by cultural conventions, while expository text structures are more variable and ill-defined. Thus, children can use their story schema to enhance their story comprehension; no such generic knowledge is available for expository prose. Finally, stories are more concrete, with events and characters that the child can identify with, through experience or imagination. Expository material, on the other hand, is typically abstract, dealing with unfamiliar concepts and situations. In summary, since understanding is highly dependent on prior knowledge and experience, we should expect to find that young children have better comprehension of narrative than expository prose.

Our discussion will conclude with a brief introduction to a new area of investigation, alluded to previously, that has important implications for educators: metacognition. Metacognition refers to the knowledge or awareness people have about cognitive processes (e.g., memory, attention, comprehension, communication). A number of experiments have shown that young children are deficient in a variety of metacognitive skills (Brown, 1975; Brown, in press; Flavell, 1978; Flavell & Wellman, 1977). For example, we noted previously that children seem to lack metacognitive knowledge about importance and logical organization (Brown & Smiley, 1977; Danner, 1976). But of more direct consequence to comprehension instruction is the growing evidence that young children have poor "metacomprehension" skills; that is, they do not always know when they don't understand. A recent study by Markman (1977) provides a good demonstration of this phenomenon. Children in grades one through three were given instructions on how to play a game or perform a magic trick. In both cases, information was left out that was critical to being able to follow the instructions. After listening to the instructions, the children were asked a series of questions designed to get them to indicate that they didn't understand. The children were told that their help was needed in coming up with good instructions, and they should let the experimenter know if something was omitted or was not clear.

The older children asked questions much more readily than the younger, realizing that the instructions were incomplete. It was often not until the first graders actually tried to carry out the instructions that they realized they didn't understand. Markman concluded that this metacomprehension failure occurred because first graders did not execute the instructions mentally as they listened to them. Although their passive listening may have given them a feeling of understanding, because they didn't actively evaluate whether the instructions made sense, they didn't know they didn't understand. In this experiment, then, children as young as third grade showed good metacomprehension. However, when the task demands are more complex, even college students are not very good at monitoring their comprehension (Baker, 1978).

These data suggest that keeping track of the state of one's comprehension during reading may be crucial to comprehension. This implies that poor comprehenders may benefit from metacomprehension training. Furthermore, it suggests that efforts should be made to teach metacomprehension skills in parallel with comprehension skills rather than waiting until remediation is necessary. At present, it seems that teachers do much of the metacognitive work for children (Wertsch, 1978); the burden should be shifted to the children themselves. We expect that further research will reveal that increasing children's awareness of their ongoing comprehension processes enhances their comprehension skills.

The preparation of this chapter was supported by the National Institute of Education under Contract No. US-NIE-C-400-76-0116. The authors would like to thank Susan Goldman, Glenn Kleiman, Carol Santa, John Santa, and Thomas Trabasso for their helpful comments on earlier versions of the chapter.

Improving Children's Prose Comprehension: Selected Strategies that Seem to Succeed

Joel R. Levin
and
Michael Pressley
University of Wisconsin

While struggling to find just the right words to communicate what this chapter is about, we came across Gordon Bower's introductory remarks in a recent article on what it takes to understand a story. Since his words reflect our thoughts, we will apply the "law of least effort" and simply reproduce them here:

> Let us begin with the familiar observation that texts we read differ a tremendous amount in their comprehensibility and in their memorability. In fact, some are so difficult that the only memorable thing about them is how incomprehensible they were. I recall taking a literature course in college where we read James Joyce's *Finnegan's Wake* [sic] [1]; although I enjoyed the flow of words and images, I could not remember enough about what I had read in order to discuss it when I went to class the next day. The same is true today if I read experimental-fiction writers such as John Hawkes. The language and imagery is often stunning and beautiful, but I barely remember enough to know where to pick up my reading again in case I lose my bookmark. One might attribute all this to my poor memory. But on the other hand, I find I have very good memory for adventure stories and folktales, for stories like those in *Canterbury Tales, The Decameron,* for detective thrillers or simple Western-cowboy stories. Most readers or movie-goers have similar experiences. It is such observations that cause psychol-

ogists to become interested in how people understand and remember simple stories (Bower, 1976, p. 511).

Why is it that certain prose passages are easy to follow
and recall, whereas others are virtually unintelligible? Factors
including passage content and topic interest are obviously
important and cannot be ignored. Even if such factors are held
constant, however, prose passages can still be more or less
comprehensible simply as a function of the way in which the
author formats, organizes, and/or presents the prose content.
The effect of these "presentation" factors on the comprehensibility of text will be discussed here. Of equal, if not more,
importance from a practical standpoint is what a *learner* can do
to increase the likelihood that a prose passage will be comprehended and recalled. Possibilities in this domain will be discussed here as well. Thus, we will focus on two general classes
of prose-learning strategies: (1) those that authors can use to
optimize communication (i.e., *prose-dependent strategies*) and
(2) those that learners can use to optimize reception (i.e.,
processor-dependent strategies).

The expansive prose-learning literature has been dealt
with in several previous reviews, two of the most recent and
most thoughtful being those of Gagné (1978) and Reder (1980).
There is no need to retrace the same steps here. Rather, we have
selected from some of that literature and elsewhere research
that we believe has implications for enhancing the prose learning of children. Although our primary focus will be on the
middle school years (i.e., on children between ages nine and
fourteen), selected research findings derived from both older
and younger populations will be included. Such findings will be
cited chiefly for purposes of developmental comparison and
contrast, or because research conducted using children within
our targeted age range is lacking.

Why did we choose to focus on the prose learning of
children? Our primary consideration was that the work discussed in this chapter be consonant with that discussed in the
other main chapters of this volume, namely the development of
comprehension skills in children (Baker & Stein) and the use of

comprehension-related curricular materials in schools (Johnson & Barrett). Although a veritable plethora of prose-learning strategies have been investigated in adolescent and adult populations (primarily high school and college students), there are obvious cognitive-developmental differences between older and younger students. Because of these differences, we believe it unwise to conclude that strategies found to be effective at one developmental level will be similarly effective at another.

Consider, for example, the strategy of having students focus on topic-related questions while reading a prose passage. This particular strategy has commanded considerable research attention in the past decade, and its potential for enhancing the prose comprehension of older students has been amply detailed (see, for example, Anderson & Biddle, 1975; Frase, 1975; and Rothkopf, 1972). A similar conclusion is not justified from the small amount of question-asking research that has been conducted with children, however. For example, the typical adult finding that questions placed just after a portion of text facilitate students' subsequent recall of prose content (including material not explicitly questioned) has not consistently emerged in studies involving children (e.g., Fischer, 1973; Richmond, 1976; Rowls, 1976; Watts, 1973).

Analogous developmental differences may be found in studies where subject-generated visual imagery constitutes the prose-learning strategy of interest. Although there is good reason to believe that such a strategy produces prose comprehension gains in children eight years of age and older (Levin, 1976; Pressley, 1977), on the basis of research conducted in our laboratory over the past few years (Dunham & Levin, 1979; Guttmann, Levin & Pressley, 1977; Ruch & Levin, 1979), the same cannot be concluded for children younger than this. Thus, we believe that inferences about the effect of various prose-learning strategies must be made with reference to the age range on which the research was based. As far as our present orientation is concerned, one is simply not justified in extrapolating downward or upward to students in the middle school years from studies conducted with older and younger students respectively (see also Levin & Lesgold, 1978).

In summary, then, in this chapter we report on strategies that seem to hold promise for facilitating children's prose learning. Our basic emphases may be reiterated in the following two questions:

1. What strategies can be applied by an author or instructor to enhance the comprehensibility and memorability of the information in a prose passage?

2. What strategies can be applied by a child who is reading or listening to the passage in order to accomplish the same thing?

These two questions should sound familiar to those who are acquainted with our previous writings (Levin, 1972, 1976; Pressley, 1977), inasmuch as they serve to evoke the distinction between what we have called *imposed* and *induced* learning strategies. This distinction will provide us with a convenient framework for organizing the present chapter.

General Framework for the Strategies Considered

Facilitative prose-learning strategies can be imposed by a communicator (Question 1 above), induced in a processor (Question 2), or both. The "both" implies that such strategies need not be mutually exclusive and, indeed, certain strategies that we will consider contain elements of each. For example, an author may include a summary at the end of a chapter to help the reader consolidate the previously presented information. This would be an imposed strategy or, in the present context, what we earlier referred to as a prose-dependent strategy. On the other hand, readers may be required to write a brief synopsis of what was just read, summarize it in their own words, review mentally the most important information, etc. Such strategies are induced in that they require some kind of relevant cognitive activity generated from *within* the learner. With these processor-dependent strategies, the onus is on the reader to perform—to give and not just to receive. Finally, as was implied above, certain strategies may be both prose- and processor-dependent. Consider, for example, a prose passage that is followed by short-answer review questions. The questions are prose dependent inasmuch as they are externally provided adjuncts to the written prose and, presumably, they are structured to consolidate in the reader's memory the information previously presented. At the same time, however, review questions are processor dependent since it is clear that whether or not they function as intended depends on the use made of them by the reader. That is, the author's objective in including such questions would obviously be frustrated if the reader did not expend the effort necessary to answer them (correctly).

Many, if not most, prose-learning strategies are both prose- and processor-dependent, and this should be realized at the outset. In our attempt to compartmentalize them, however, we are forced to make some "either/or" decisions about strategies, based on whether a particular strategy appears to us as either *predominantly* prose dependent or processor dependent. Although we are reluctant to dichotomize strategies in this fashion, by doing so our strategy classifications and discussion become more manageable.

We turn, then, to Table 1 where exemplars of our present emphases are presented. The row levels, of course, represent the

Table 1
Four Classes of Prose-Comprehension Strategy, as Represented
by Assumed Primary Function and Type

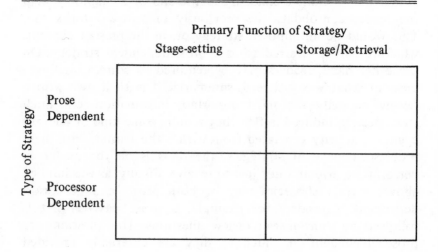

	Primary Function of Strategy	
	Stage-setting	Storage/Retrieval
Prose Dependent		
Processor Dependent		

Levin and Pressley

two classes of prose-learning strategies just considered. A second dimension to our framework is afforded by the two column labels. That is, strategy types (prose- or processor-dependent) can be further broken down according to their assumed primary function in a prose-learning context. As will be seen, these functions loosely correspond to the particular point in time that the strategy is applied: prior to, as opposed to during, passage presentation.[2]

We are inclined to view the general class of prose-learning strategies that are activated *prior to* passage presentation as serving primarily a *context-* or *stage-setting* function. That is, they sensitize the student to what the passage is about, what should be learned from it, what existing information the student already possesses concerning the material, and the like. In contrast, prose-learning strategies activated *during* passage presentation will be regarded as serving an information *storage/retrieval* function. Although *both* strategy types discussed here are, to some extent, concerned with storage and retrieval (and, in particular, with facilitating storage and retrieval), those applied during passage presentation operate on prose information directly and in its presence. Examples include alternative structural and logical text organizations (see Baker & Stein, this volume), the provision of content-clarifying auxiliary materials, and student-generated cognitive elaborations and transformations of passage content.

As mentioned earlier, our general plan in this chapter is to provide the reader with examples of children's prose-comprehension strategies that "seem to succeed." These examples are just that: illustrations and not exhaustive listings.[3] Our presentation of the various examples will now follow from the four cells represented in Table 1.

Examples of Seemingly Successful Children's Prose-Comprehension Strategies

Stage-Setting Strategies

PROSE-DEPENDENT, STAGE-SETTING STRATEGIES

Whether contained in the prose materials or provided by

an instructor, our stage-setting strategies encompass the kinds of "preinstructional strategies" recently reviewed by Hartley and Davies (1976). Included are question answering (pretests), instructional objectives ("goals" and "purposes"), overviews, and Ausubelian "advance organizers" (Ausubel, 1963). The first two strategies may be regarded as primarily *sensitizing* or "orienting" (Frase, 1970) in nature, in that they may introduce terms or hint at to-be-learned content and skills, but they do not inform per se. Of course, the hope is that when such sensitizers are combined with the subsequent prose content, learning will be enhanced (possibly as a result of increased attention paid to particular terms and ideas when they are encountered in the text). The success of sensitization strategies, with respect to the *specific material sensitized,* has been fairly well established with students of all ages. In short, alerting students to exactly what it is they are to learn is generally more effective than "leaving them in the dark"—not very surprising, perhaps, but often overlooked in instructional practice.

The second two of the Hartley and Davies (1976) preinstructional strategies are basically *content-clarifying* and, therefore, informational in their own right. It is worth mentioning that previous distinctions (and arguments about distinctions) between overviews and advance organizers appear throughout the literature (Barnes & Clawson, 1975; Lawton & Wanska, 1977), and we do not wish to fuel the fire here. That is, we will not debate what the salient characteristics of a good advance organizer, as conceived by Ausubel, are (e.g., consists of a higher "level of abstraction," provides a needed "ideational scaffolding," etc.), in contrast to those of a good overview. Rather than belabor the issue, we will regard both overviews and organizers as content-clarifying preinstructional strategies, and use the terms more or less interchangeably. Certainly as far as the prose comprehension of children is concerned, we subscribe to the view that content-clarifying preinstructional strategies (of whichever type) should be relatively simple and concrete. We further believe that such simplification or concretization strategies will exhibit their greatest payoffs on prose passages whose content is far from simple or concrete. We will return to both of these points following an illustration of the kind of strategy we have in mind.

Arnold and Brooks (1976). A number of adult studies have demonstrated that prose learning proceeds much more efficiently once an appropriate organizing context has been established (i.e., once the stage has been properly set). Of particular significance to the present discussion, Bransford and Johnson (1973) have found that students' understanding and recall of an otherwise difficult-to-comprehend prose passage was helped considerably by the provision of either a stage-setting visual illustration or a verbal title. Arnold and Brooks sought to replicate and extend the Bransford and Johnson findings using second and fifth grade children. What follows is one of the eight short passages created by Arnold and Brooks:

> Jimmy was hanging by his knees and his legs were beginning to ache, but he still hung on. The swan was flying very fast towards Jimmy's home. The wind was blowing through Jimmy's hair and jacket and he was getting cold. The other children were having a good time. Jimmy wished the trip were over. Lisa had fallen asleep on the white feather mattress and Joey was singing a song (Arnold & Brooks, 1976, p. 712).

Although each individual sentence is easily comprehended—even by a child—the passage formed by the collection of sentences is not likely to be—even by an adult. What seems to be missing is a meaningful context, or theme, within which the individual sentences can be embedded.

Just prior to listening to each passage, children in one condition were provided with a theme, in the form of a stage-setting illustration. One such illustration is provided here as Panel A of Figure 1. (How does this information affect your reinterpretation of the previous passage?) In a control condition, children were shown a random arrangement of the same elements of the illustration (Panel B of Figure 1) just prior to the presentation of the story. This condition was derived from Bransford and Johnson (1972), and was designed to control for everything except the explicit context in the experimental condition.

Selecting Strategies   51

Figure 1. Example of organized (A) and control (B) pictorial stage-setting contexts. (Taken from Arnold & Brooks, 1976; copyright 1976 by the American Psychological Association; reprinted by permission.)

If an appropriate *context* is related to comprehension and recall of a prose passage (as suggested by the adult research), then performance differences between the two conditions would be expected. Based on a subsequent free-recall measure of information derived exclusively from the passage, this was indeed found to be the case for fifth grade children: Those who received the integrated context recalled almost one-third more passage content than did control students. Thus, the same sort of stage-setting illustrations that improve the prose learning of adults (Bransford & Johnson, 1972) also seem to succeed with children as young as fifth graders. The Arnold and Brooks data do not permit the conclusion that children younger than this will exhibit similar improvements, since in that study the second graders did not appear to benefit from the preinstructional organizer.[4] This latter finding is but one instance of our introductory caution against making blanket across-age generalizations.

Related remarks. In addition to the two pictorial conditions described in the preceding section, Arnold and Brooks included two similar (though less specific) purely *verbal* conditions in their experiment. These consisted of informing students just prior to passage presentation either that the story was about "two boys and a girl riding a swan" (Context) or that it was about "two boys and a girl *and* a swan" (Control). Based on the passage-recall measure discussed previously, no significant increase in the performance of context students, relative to controls, was apparent at either grade level (the increase was only about 6 percent among fifth graders). Why should the pictorial organizer be effective and the verbal organizer not, when it comes to recalling passage content? Surely these two organizer types differ in many respects (including the greater specificity of the pictorial organizer, as may be appreciated from a look at Figure 1), but it cannot be denied that the provided illustration affords a very simple, concrete framework for organizing the incoming passage content. As we argued before concerning content-clarifying preinstructional strategies, they should be easy to follow and concrete. One of the best ways to satisfy these criteria is to provide a compact pictorial organizer. Although we are not denying the possibility of devising similarly effective verbal organizers, it seems unlikely that even the ultimate "thousand-word" treatise will be "worth" perceptibly more than a compact "one-picture" organizer.

Our second previously stated belief about content-clarifying preinstructional strategies is that they should become particularly effective when the "going gets rough." What this means is that the benefits derived from content-clarifying organizers should be greatest with difficult-to-comprehend passages. "Difficult," as applied here, is only vaguely defined, but is a concept that can be easily operationalized in relative terms. For example, the thematically barren passages of Arnold and Brooks (1976) could be mixed with comparable, though thematically rich, passages and read to students for comprehension-difficulty ratings (see Bransford & Johnson, 1972). If our speculations about organizer effectiveness are on target, then it should be the case that content-clarifying organizers would be comparatively more beneficial for the subsequent recall of passages rated more difficult to comprehend. An alternative way to evaluate these speculations would be to examine the effectiveness of content-clarifying organizers using prose passages of varying abstractness.

It is fairly well established that learning materials (prose passages included) which deal primarily with abstract referents and events are less well comprehended and recalled in comparison to learning materials focussing on concrete referents and events (M. Johnson, Bransford, Nyberg, & Cleary, 1972; R. Johnson, 1974). [We are using the terms "concrete" and "abstract" in the contemporary psychological sense here to refer to stimuli that are rated as being more and less tangible/visualizable, respectively (see Paivio, 1971).] Thus, we would predict that content-clarifying organizers would be especially helpful for children in situations where the passage content was relatively abstract. Although little, if any, systematic data bearing *directly* on this prediction seem to be available, a few studies based on adults lend indirect support to it (see Davidson, 1976 and Royer & Cable, 1976). In these studies students' comprehension of very abstract prose passages was helped by instructor-provided concrete organizers.

PROCESSOR-DEPENDENT, STAGE-SETTING STRATEGIES

We turn now to the second of our stage-setting strategies as represented in Table 1. Here, organizing information relevant to the upcoming passage must be called into play by the prose processor. The most usual application of this strategy is for students to relate what they anticipate the passage will be about to what they already know. In a phrase, relevant "knowledge of the world" is activated by students in order to comprehend better (or even at all) the to-be-learned prose material.

Consider, as a simple analogical manifestation of this kind of strategy, the television game show, "The $20,000 Pyramid," which we watch regularly to get ideas about comprehension, communication, and how people think. In the first segment of each contest, the player must identify category members when given clues about those members by his or her partner. For example, suppose the category were "French things" and one's partner were to say: "A very tall structure, trademark of Paris, built for a World Fair." (Of course the answer desired is *Eiffel Tower*.) During the time allotted for a given game (30 seconds), a contestant must identify seven different exemplars from a given category (e.g., seven different "French things"). Thus, time is at a premium. It turns out that a very good (and very obvious) pregame, stage-setting strategy that contestants can employ is to focus their attention on the particular category, and to start activating their existing knowledge structures within that category in order to *anticipate* exemplars that might be requested. What follows is a strategic contestant's plausible self-dialogue (exaggerated, of course, since only a few seconds of preparation time are allowed):

> Now let's see, the category is "French things." What do I know that's French? Food things (a popular first choice): French fries, French onion soup, vichyssoise, maitre d', cabernet sauvignon, escargots, quiche lorraine, Cuisinart. What else around here? Renaults, French poodles, Brigitte Bardot, Truffaut, Jacques Cousteau, Jean Claude Killy, the French Alps. What about in France? The River Seine, Paris, Arc de Triomphe, Eiffel Tower, Notre Dame, The Louvre, Toulouse Lautrec, impressionism. What else? Napoleon Bonaparte, Joan of Arc, . . .OK, let's go.

A similar type of strategic anticipation can come into play when processing text and to paraphrase a familiar saying: What one brings into a prose passage often determines what one will take out. (Just take a crack at *Finnegans Wake*, for example —see also Footnote 1.) However, the processor-dependent, stage-setting strategy cell of Table 1 is a maverick of sorts. Frankly, it was born purely out of "slot-filling" necessity in order to provide some (literal) balance to our prose-comprehension framework.[5] We will now attempt to explain why we view this particular cell as a forced entry, but a forced entry that is important to consider when discussing prose-learning strategies.

First, it is often the case with prose that no stage-setting clues are provided concerning passage/topic content, and even when they are they may be too vague (for a student to operate on them effectively) or unhelpful (if the stage-setting clues do not trigger off the student's preexisting related knowledge). Second, and partly because of the above, the stage-setting strategies *applied by a processor* are bound to be much less purposive (i.e., applied with less intention) than is connoted by our use of the term "strategy" throughout this chapter. Thus, we apply the term "strategy" to the processor-dependent, stage-setting cell of Table 1 with some reluctance.[6]

A few preliminary remarks are in order. There is ample theoretical discussion, and corroborative empirical evidence, relevant to the notion that one's prior knowledge predicts one's perception, comprehension, and recall of "new" information (Anderson et al., 1977, Footnote 5). Brief mention of an interesting recent study by Gordon, Hansen, and Pearson (1978) will suffice to make the point here. These authors found that young (second grade) children who had some prior knowledge about a given topic ("spiders") learned more from those portions of a "spider" passage *where that prior knowledge could be applied,* relative to children who had little or no prior "spider" knowledge. In contrast, for information explicitly stated in the passage and for which no prior "spider" knowledge was necessary, the two groups of children did not differ significantly with respect to amount learned.

As far as processor-dependent strategies are concerned, it is easy to make a mockery of the prior-knowledge-predicts-present-learning principle: Simply provide students with as much background knowledge *as possible*—before giving them additional related material to learn (Levin, 1978). But surely the less extreme recommendation that follows from the principle is not so ridiculous: Simply provide students with as much background knowledge *as is necessary* to facilitate comprehension of the to-be-learned material. This less extreme prescription has in fact been proffered to reading practitioners (Betts, 1957, p. 494), and is well illustrated, we believe, in an experiment reported by Brown, Smiley, Day, Townsend, & Lawton (1977, Exp. 2).

Brown et al. (1977). In this experiment, second, fourth, and sixth graders were asked to listen to a passage about a hunter from the fictitious "Targa" tribe. Although certain details of the passage were left unspecified, the passage itself was perfectly comprehensible in its presented form (unlike that of Arnold & Brooks, 1976). However, in an attempt to influence students' interpretation of the passage, Brown et al. manipulated the children's background knowledge of the Targa the week before the passage was actually presented. One group of children was informed that Targas were of the peaceful Eskimo variety, and details (both pictorial and verbal) such as snow-related settings, polar wildlife, and all the "trappings" were provided for students to embellish this orientation. A second group of children was given a warring Indian orientation, along with burning deserts, water and animal shortages, etc. A third (control) group was given information about Spanish people the week before, which was of course irrelevant to the ensuing Targa-target passage. (For further description of this experiment, see Baker & Stein, this volume.)

Two findings are of particular note. First, the two groups with preestablished background knowledge about the Targa recalled over 25 percent more passage content than controls. Second, convincing evidence was provided to show that the different kinds of relevant background information (Eskimo vs. Indian) did influence students' processing of the passage. In particular, the recall errors that were made were consistent with children's preestablished backgrounds: About two-thirds of all recall errors consisted of appropriate background information that was *not* in fact mentioned in the passage; that is, Eskimo-oriented students "recalled" Eskimo-related information that was not there, whereas unmentioned Indian-related background information was "recalled" by Indian-oriented students. The same pattern was apparent in some follow-up questions designed to determine whether specific background information did, in fact, influence the children's interpretation of the passage.

Related remarks. Gordon et al.'s research (1978) has demonstrated that young children's existing knowledge about a particular topic may determine what and how much they will learn from a prose passage containing new topic-related information. From a methodological standpoint this is important inasmuch as it highlights the claims of others (Levin & Lesgold, 1978; Royer & Cunningham, 1978) that if one is interested in assessing strictly what a student has *learned* from a prose passage, then what the student already *knows*—or can deduce without even reading the passage—must first be taken into account. From a substantive standpoint the finding suggests that if relevant knowledge structures are well established, learning will proceed more efficiently. Brown et al.'s experimental demonstration (1977, Exp. 2) is in accord with this position, as is a study with adults reported by Davidson (1976). The Davidson study will be described here in some detail since it is a good example of how prior knowledge can make comprehensible otherwise very difficult-to-comprehend material.

Davidson selected "The Mat Maker" chapter from Melville's *Moby Dick* as the to-be-learned prose content. Given our earlier comments about stage-setting strategies likely being more helpful for comparatively difficult and/or abstract passages, "The Mat Maker" certainly is a prime candidate for facilitation. As the reader may recall from his or her own experiences with this passage, a number of abstract concepts (such as fate, chance, and free will) are interrelated, to each other as well as metaphorically to various concrete parts of a loom (such as the warp, the woof, and the shuttle). It goes without saying that one's background familarity with looms should predict how well Melville's analogies should "work" (as with the Gordon et al., 1978, "spider" study).

Realizing this, and by selecting learners with presumably "loomless" backgrounds (in contrast to weavers—see Anderson, Reynolds, Schallert, & Goetz, 1977, for an interesting variation on this theme), Davidson attempted to fill in the needed "loom" network by preinstructing one group of students as to the nature of the loom and its working parts. Both pictures and verbal descriptions were used in this loom-knowledge phase.

On the subsequent passage, Davidson found that the students with built-up loom backgrounds outperformed two groups of control students on a true-false assertion test. Compared to the two control groups combined, loom-knowledge students correctly identified almost 50 percent more items. In addition, qualitative analyses of free-recall protocols of the students revealed quite different structurings of passage information in the loom-knowledge and control conditions. Loom-knowledge students were found to be much more likely to relate abstract concepts from the passage to concrete loom parts, relative to control students who tended to maintain separate abstract and concrete concept clusters.

In reviewing the literature on content-clarifying strategies in the stage-setting domain (Arnold & Brooks, 1976; Brown et al., 1977; Davidson, 1976), the present authors have come to believe in the utility of such strategies—but within limits. A few of these limits were specified earlier. For example, it appears that organizers and background knowledge facilitate students' comprehension of difficult-to-comprehend (abstract, unfamiliar, or ambiguous) material. This is intuitively pleasing and seems to have modest empirical support. After all, why *should* stage-setting information be needed if the upcoming passage is concrete, familiar, and straightforward? At the same time, it is reasonable to suppose that *extremely* difficult-to-comprehend passages (and/or organizers) would diminish stage-setting effects. Moreover, this supposition may be of special importance when the students are cognitively less advanced, as evidenced by reported facilitation breakdowns when elementary school children have been presented with preinstructional organizers for difficult passages (e.g., the second graders of

Arnold & Brooks, 1976; Hawkins, 1971).

Storage/Retrieval Strategies

As was mentioned in the introduction, storage/retrieval strategies (as we have defined them) encompass the class of adjuncts and information-processing activities that can be brought into play during passage presentation (i.e., in the company of the to-be-learned text). Our initial reference to Bower's introspective excursions with Chaucer (1976) in contrast to James Joyce could serve as a testimony to the very different perceived means by which a text's structure and/or content can be organized. Baker and Stein (this volume) and Shimmerlik (1978) provide recent reviews of relevant passage-organization variables, and these will not be duplicated here. Suffice it to say that 1) better-organized prose passages are generally better learned as well and 2) how a passage is organized generally determines what prose content students will learn and how they will organize that content. In this section we consider illustrative strategies that seem to render a given prose content and/or structure more memorable for children.

PROSE-DEPENDENT, STORAGE/RETRIEVAL STRATEGIES

Apart from providing an efficient structuring of the prose content that is there, a communicator can alter or add to the form in which that content is presented. Altering the form of a prose passage includes typographical/formatting changes (Frase, 1977) and modality/media alternatives to *reading* per se, such as listening to a live lecture or a tape, watching a movie or dramatization, and various multimedia explorations (see, for example, almost any recent issue of the *AV Communication Review*— now, *Educational Communication and Technology*). Adding to a prose passage's form includes communicator-inserted aids designed to facilitate storage and retrieval of the prose content, such as the use of topic sentences, appropriate headings and emphases, and marginal comments (Browning, 1976; Dee-Lucas & Di Vesta, 1978; Doctorow, Wittrock, & Marks, 1978; Wilkie, 1978).

A personal trilogy (1977–1978). We wish to include as an

(literal) illustration of a prose-dependent, storage/retrieval strategy one that definitely seems to succeed with children (and, for that matter, with adults as well). This is the strategy of inserting visual illustrations (pictures) into a prose passage to convey the essence of the content (for recent reviews documenting the success of this strategy, see Levin, in press; Levin & Lesgold, 1978; Pressley, 1977; and Schallert, 1980). The "personal trilogy" aspect of this illustration comes from the fact that we will cite three recent studies from our own laboratory which adequately represent the strategy (Bender & Levin, 1978; Guttmann et al., 1977; and Ruch & Levin, 1977).

In each of these studies, children were read 10- to 20-sentence narrative passages, either in the company or absence of content-capturing colored line drawings. Each sentence of the passage had its own associated picture that was displayed while the sentence was read. Following passage presentation, the children were asked a series of short answer ("Wh") questions, constructed so as to be highly "passage dependent" (Tuinman, 1973–1974). By this is meant that it was very unlikely that students could respond correctly to the questions without having first been exposed to the passage. Thus, we can be quite certain that the data from these studies represent learning from text, rather than pure prior knowledge of the world or test-wiseness.

To make the preceding comments more concrete, consider the initial sentence from one of the passages (Guttmann et al., 1977): *One evening Sue's family sat down to eat a big turkey for dinner.* The picture accompanying this sentence is shown as Panel A of Figure 2, and a question related to the content is: *What did Sue's family eat for dinner one evening?* It can be stated that the correct answer, *turkey,* is not likely to be supplied by students who are asked the question without their first having heard the passage, since sentences and questions were constructed on the basis of just such "norming" information. That is, students who are asked to provide a reasonable answer to this question out of context typically respond with *hamburgers, hotdogs,* or *soup.* Nonetheless, whether or not students who heard the passage and correctly answered the

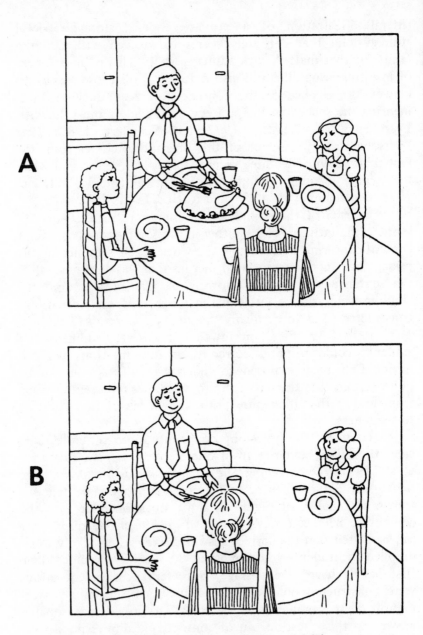

Figure 2. Examples of complete (A) and partial (B) pictures.

Levin and Pressley

question actually *comprehended* what they heard is a matter we will consider shortly.

The basic datum of present interest is that in each of these studies, children who heard the story in the company of pictures recalled substantially more prose information in comparison to children who simply heard the story without pictures. In the Guttmann et al. (1977) study, kindergartners, first graders, and third graders experienced gains due to pictures of about 43 percent, 36 percent, and 39 percent respectively. From these figures, it can be seen that the intuitive notion that pictures are likely to be relatively more helpful for younger children than for older children is not supported, since the facilitation percentages are comparable at all grade levels (see Levin's 1976 discussion related to picture effects in general). In the Bender and Levin (1978) study using a longer passage, third graders increased their recall by over 25 percent when pictures were provided; and for the main target group of that study—educable mental retardates between ages ten and sixteen —the increase was 89 percent! Clearly, performance gains of this magnitude cannot be regarded as trivial.

These studies appear to be significant in at least two other respects. First, it will be noted from Panel A of Figure 2 that the information asked for in the question (i.e., *turkey*) is physically present in the picture. In contrast, because of their interest in visual imagery and its presumed development in prose-learning situations, Guttmann et al. and Ruch and Levin (1977) fashioned illustrated contexts ("partial pictures") in which the to-be-supplied information was strongly suggested by, though not physically present in, the provided picture. (See, for example, Panel B of Figure 2, where a perspective-blocking tactic was adopted.) Students who were presented these partial pictures were told to use what was displayed in the picture to help them construct an image of what was not displayed. As was previously noted for text-embedded questions, such a strategy can be seen to involve both prose-dependent elements (here, author-illustrated contexts) and processor-dependent elements (listener-imagined content). In the case of partial pictures it is assumed that the pictorial contexts "prompt"

(Rohwer, 1973) the appropriate visual imagery. Interestingly for present purposes, partial pictures were found to increase children's prose recall (by about 30 percent). As far as prose-dependent strategies per se are concerned, the important point is that even less-than-complete pictures (if appropriately constructed)[7] can function as effective children's prose-learning aids (see also Riding & Shore, 1974).

The second significant aspect of the studies being considered here is some evidence provided concerning the nature of information processing associated with communicator-provided pictures. It has been argued previously that short-answer questions should consist of paraphrases of the original passage content in order to increase one's chances of measuring *comprehension* rather than simple rote recall (Anderson, 1972). Thus, in contrast to the earlier given *verbatim* question about what Sue and her family were eating for dinner, a *paraphrase* question could be stated as: *What food was served at the girl's house at suppertime?* Consistent with theoretical notions about the verbatim-paraphrase distinction, it has been found that simple rote repetition of passage content is sufficient to produce facilitated performance on verbatim-worded questions (Blank & Frank, 1971; Levin, Bender, & Lesgold, 1976). On the other hand, provided pictures and partial pictures have been found to facilitate performance with *both* verbatim and paraphrase questions (Bender & Levin, 1978; Levin et al., 1976; Peng & Levin, 1979; Ruch & Levin, 1977). In the Levin et al. study, for example, pictures were superior to simple repetition for first graders' performance on verbatim questions; in the Ruch and Levin study, partial pictures improved the performance of third graders on both verbatim and paraphrase questions, whereas simple repetition was effective only for the former (presumed less comprehension-demanding) question variation; and in the Bender and Levin study, pictures facilitated retardates' performance again on both question variations, whereas simple repetition did not facilitate performance on either type. Such findings are important insofar as they lend support to the argument that pictures do more than simple repetition in the way of promoting increased comprehension of prose content. (See

Levin, in press, and Levin and Lesgold, 1978, for additional comments about what pictures in prose can and cannot be expected to accomplish.)

The final cell of Table 1 is the one in which there is ongoing activity *on the part of the prose processor* to store the passage information in a manner that is effective for subsequent retrieval. Based on a review of the relevant empirical literature, it seems safe to conclude that the kind of activities likely to be successful prose-comprehension strategies are those which require personal "cognitive constructions." Although cognitive constructions have been variously referred to by others in the past, we take these to include those mental operations of a processor that are aimed at (re)organizing and/or elaborating upon the prose content. Strategies such as constructing imaginal representations of textual information, responding to questions that require comprehension-level processing of the prose content, and generating paraphrases of the information just processed have all been identified as effective strategies with children (Doctorow et al., 1978; Guttmann et al., 1977; Yost, Avila, & Vexler, 1977). Other cognitive-constructive activity such as underlining of perceived important content and note taking could also be considered, but they are neither well-established successes nor well-studied with children (Anderson, 1980; Brown & Smiley, 1978; Browning, 1976).[8] Let us consider here an example of a processor-dependent, storage/retrieval strategy that has been applied by elementary school children to yield handsome reading comprehension returns.

Doctorow et al. (1978). In this study, sixth grade students were given fairly complex passages to read (high and low readers were given different passages, appropriate for their reading level). Included in the several experimental conditions were two of concern for present purposes. Students in a paraphrase condition were required to write a sentence summarizing the content of each paragraph as they read it. It was thought that this type of activity would induce students to process the story information with greater comprehension in comparison to control students who were exposed to the passage for the same amount of time but with no paraphrasing instructions. A commendable feature of this experiment that should be highlighted is the equivalent amount of passage exposure time across treatment conditions. As a result, performance differences between conditions cannot be attributed to time and/or content repetition differences per se, as has been argued for other adjunct-to-text experiments (Ladas, 1973; Levin & Lesgold, 1978).

It was found that constructing paragraph paraphrases was an eminently manageable task for children of this age since they could do so about 80 percent of the time (no content analysis of the "quality" of the paraphrase was provided, however). Moreover, consistent with the hypothesized comprehension-inducing character of this activity, paraphrase students outperformed controls on both an immediate multiple-choice test and a delayed (by one week) modified cloze test. This was true for both high and low reading groups. Averaged across reading groups (and, thus, across passages), paraphrasing increased students' performance by over 50 percent on both tests.

Related remarks. Recent work with high school and college students supports the notion that paraphrasing (Pio & Andre, 1977) and other forms of cognitive-constructive activity (Dee-Lucas & DiVesta, 1980; Shimmerlik & Nolan, 1976) are effective prose-learning strategies. Included here is the activity of responding to text-embedded questions while reading. Given our obvious affinity for pictorial comprehension aids, an interesting study is that of Snowman and Cunningham (1975) in which it was found that both student-generated verbal responses *and* student-generated line drawings (in response to communicator-provided questions) functioned effectively and equally to improve performance.

With younger students (seventh graders), Yost et al. (1977) found that a question is *not* a question is *not* a question. Consistent with what could have been anticipated from the earlier sentence-learning findings of Watts and Anderson (1971), as well as the levels-of-processing framework of Craik and

Lockhart (1972), these authors demonstrated that questions prompting more elaborate cognitive constructions on the part of the student (i.e., questions whose answers required greater integration and synthesis of text content) produced greater learning gains in comparison to questions prompting simpler cognitive constructions. Students responding to higher-level questions also expended more time, however, which must be considered when interpreting the Yost et al. results.

Finally, a study by Brown and Smiley (1978) serves to illustrate an important chicken-and-egg problem that must frequently be wrestled with by researchers in this domain. Potentially effective prose-learning strategies are often discovered either on the basis of a researcher's intuition or from introspective reports supplied by effective prose learners (e.g., college students and precocious children). For example, in one of their experiments with fifth, seventh, and eighth grade students Brown and Smiley found that the most proficient prose learners were those who elected spontaneously to take notes and/or underline while they were reading. It might therefore be predicted that if less proficient prose learners were instructed to engage in the same kind of cognitive-constructive activity, their prose-learning performance would exhibit an increase. Instructing students to generate visual images to represent the content of concrete narrative passages has proven successful in this regard (Levin, 1972, 1976; and Pressley, 1977). In the Brown and Smiley experiment, however, the less proficient prose learners did *not* benefit from a preinstructional suggestion to take notes and/or underline. This is not surprising, given that such students were found to produce notes and underlinings of inferior quality. Thus, the experiment helps to make the point that simply instructing a less proficient prose learner to adopt a strategy spontaneously applied by a more proficient prose learner will not always be sufficient to effect a comprehension increase. In fairness to note taking and underlining, however, it should be mentioned that in the Brown and Smiley experiment no explicit instruction was provided concerning *how* to take notes and underline effectively. Indeed, the request for students to apply the strategies was given as little more than a hint that it would be permissible for them to do so.

Reflections on Research into Children's Prose-Comprehension Strategies

We conclude this chapter by reflecting on a couple of general feelings that were evoked during the course of our perusal of the children's prose-learning literature. One general feeling we had was that a vast number of prose-processing activities have the *potential* to be effective strategies for children. Whether or not a particular strategy realizes its potential, however, depends on a host of situational factors. These factors include both prose characteristics (e.g., difficulty and concreteness, as discussed earlier in this chapter) and processor characteristics (e.g., the student's cognitive-developmental level). Unfortunately, however, researchers typically select the specific prose passages and students for their experiments on the basis of convenience rather than on the basis of substantive or theoretical considerations. An informed guess is that the mixed results and nonreplications that crop up in the prose-learning literature may be traced to just such unconsidered choices.

For these reasons we believe that quests for the single "best" prose-learning strategy are not likely to be productive. Because of the situational constraints alluded to above, it is not at all surprising that one researcher's "champ" turns out to be another's "chump" as far as effective prose-learning strategies go. We want to reiterate our earlier comments (including Footnote 2) that we have not exhaustively surveyed the many prose-learning strategies that have been studied by educational researchers. In particular, we are well aware that other researchers believe in "champs" that differ from those included here (e.g., the Ausubelians and the many researchers in the Rothkopf, 1970, "mathemagenics" tradition). We regret that we were unable to give their candidates more attention in this chapter. Nonetheless, we are convinced that the strategies illustrated here will prove to be important educationally.

Another general feeling we walked away from the literature with was that there is tremendous variability in the apparent effectiveness of strategy *implementation* from one study to the next. By this is meant that one must pay close attention to the thoughtfulness and thoroughness with which a particular strategy is administered in any particular study. To say that a "paraphrase" or "note-taking" strategy was employed by so and so et al. is simply not sufficient. Attention to implementation details is mandatory. In the case of prose-dependent strategies, one should ask how crudely or how elaborately they were represented, and whether in fact they conveyed what they purported to convey. (We are reminded here of the Arnold and Brooks, 1976, verbal organizer, among others.) In the case of processor-dependent strategies, one should ask what and how much systematic instruction (including practice and examples) was provided for students prior to allowing them to launch out on their own. (We are reminded here of the Brown and Smiley, 1978, hint to take notes and/or underline, among others.) As has been argued previously in the context of evaluating innovative educational programs, one must be careful not to confuse the issue of whether a program "worked" with whether it was implemented as intended. Obviously, failure of the latter would preclude success of the former.

In this sense, it must also be realized that prose-learning strategies of the processor variety are surely not going to fulfill their promise unless a fair amount of dedication and old-fashioned hard work are invested by the student who is employing them. For example, the few attempts to provide children with extended instruction in the use of a visual imagery strategy have not yielded overly impressive returns (Pressley, 1976), especially when the children are transferred to slightly different contexts (Lesgold, McCormick, & Golinkoff, 1975; Triplett, 1980).[9] Although we remain hopeful that training programs designed to improve children's prose learning will constitute a viable (and perhaps even vital) prescription for many children and other inefficient prose processors, what must be considered more carefully are the boundary conditions associated with a particular strategy's effectiveness. The questions of when and with whom any given strategy will be effective are terribly important ones. We have alluded to numerous likely boundary conditions throughout this chapter, and Levin (in press) considers the case of visual imagery in particular.

In the final analysis, potentially effective prose-learning strategies require clever delivery on the part of an instructor (including the matching of strategies to materials and students), and conscientious application of the selected strategy on the part of the student. Only then will the pain of learning bring about the joy of having learned.

Footnotes

The work represented here was funded by the Wisconsin Research and Development Center for Individualized Schooling, supported in part as a research and development center by funds from the National Institute of Education (Center No. NE-C-00-3-0065). The opinions herein do not necessarily reflect the position or policy of the National Institute of Education and no official endorsement by the National Institute of Education should be inferred. The second author is now at the Department of Psychology, University of Western Ontario. We are grateful to Kay Camperell, Joseph Lawton, and Jean Padrutt for their helpful comments and to Lynn Sowle for typing the manuscript.

[1] An aside to the highbrow: What's wrong with this title? (Answer to be provided later in this chapter.)

[2] Time-tied classifications of prose-learning adjuncts and activities have been adopted by others as well (Anderson, 1980; Carroll, 1971; Gagné, 1978). Moreover, there are effective information-consolidation activities that can be applied *following* a prose passage, such as review quizzes of various kinds and with various types of information feedback (see Anderson & Biddle, 1975; and Kulhavy, 1977). Test-taking "strategies" will not be considered here, however, and activities such as summarizing or reviewing a prose passage will be regarded as during-prose strategies for present purposes.

[3] The term "illustrations" is used here in both the literal and figurative sense, if the reader will excuse an inverted double pun. "Literal" illustrations will be taken from children's prose-learning studies in which the strategies consist of prose-dependent *pictures* and processor-dependent *visual imagery*. On the other hand, "figurative" illustrations will be taken from the same sort of studies, but in which the strategies are nonpictorial in nature. We alert the reader that as a consequence of our own experiences (and biases) associated with children's prose-learning research, our emphasis in this chapter will clearly be on the former (literal) type of illustrations.

[4] These conclusions are based on the summary data supplied by Arnold and Brooks, and it is clear that our interpretation of their data differs from their own. Without going into the specifics here, this is due to the fact that Arnold and Brooks' discussion was based primarily on analyses of what we consider to be an inappropriate performance measure. This measure ("inferences") included as correct responses certain information which was not explicitly contained in the passage and which serves unjustifiably to bias the recall data in favor of context-provided students. When one focusses strictly on students' correct recall of *passage-derived* content, about all that can be said is that fifth graders who are provided with stage-setting illustrations display a significant performance increment relative to appropriate controls.

[5] "Slot filling" is a term purposely borrowed from *schema theory* since that best elucidates the nature of the processor-dependent, stage-setting strategy cell. Anderson, Spiro, and Montague's 1977 volume is devoted to schema theory and is highly recommended. Not only is the theory's basis clearly articulated throughout, but specific educational implications of the theory follow directly from much of the work reported there (see also Baker & Stein, this volume).

[6] On the other hand, there are reading authorities who explicitly advocate the use of processor-dependent, stage-setting strategies. For instance, in reviewing texts on how to teach reading, we found numerous recommendations that teachers ought to prompt children to apply what they already know in order to improve their comprehension of upcoming text (Dechant, 1970; Spache & Spache, 1977; Stauffer, 1969; and Zintz, 1970). When viewed from this perspective, the term "strategy" might not be as ill-suited to our processor-dependent, stage-setting cell as one might think.

[7] This "appropriately constructed" proviso was motivated by the failure of other studies to detect positive effects due to pictures. The studies can be characterized by their use of pictures that were either irrelevant or only weakly related to the essential prose content, however (see Levin & Lesgold, 1978).

[8] The reader activities of previewing (skimming) and reviewing relevant portions of text could be included here as well.

[9] The multiple-strategy approaches of Dansereau and his colleagues (Dansereau, McDonald, Collins, Garland, Holley, Dickhoff, & Evans, 1979) and of Weinstein and her colleagues (1979) with older students may ultimately prove successful, but systematic data on which to evaluate them are presently either unavailable or compromised by inadequate controls. Similar comments apply to other multicomponent reading comprehension strategies, such as SQ3R (Robinson, 1961).

Prose Comprehension: A Descriptive Analysis of Instructional Practices

Dale D. Johnson
and
Thomas C. Barrett
University of Wisconsin at Madison

Other chapters in this monograph analyze and evaluate theory and research related to the comprehension of prose passages. The purpose of this chapter, however, is to examine suggested instructional practices designed to develop children's comprehension of prose passages in a selected sample of professional and instructional sources dealing with the teaching of reading. To accomplish this objective, we did four things, which in turn provided the basis for the organization of this chapter:

1. A framework of reading comprehension tasks was developed to serve as a criterion reference for examining the instructional practices found in the aforementioned sources

2. The comprehension tasks suggested in selected basal reading series were analyzed at two grade levels

3. The comprehension tasks in a set of current professional texts on the teaching of reading were examined

4. Some currently emphasized elements for instructional strategies to facilitate the comprehension of prose passages were isolated.

Before proceeding, a comment about our use of certain terms seems warranted. Comprehension pedagogy, as is true with so many facets of education, abounds with overlapping and confusing jargon. Some concepts have many labels and some labels represent different concepts. In this chapter the terms *tasks* and *strategies* are differentiated somewhat arbitrarily and, at times unevenly, by referring to things students do as comprehension *tasks* and the things the teachers do as instructional *strategies*.

A Framework of Comprehension Tasks

In order to organize our descriptive analysis of current instructional practices related to the development of children's comprehension of prose passages, we developed a framework of comprehension tasks to serve as a criterion reference for the analysis. There are, of course, a number of such frameworks available. They range from taxonomies of the cognitive domain or reading comprehension such as those proposed by Bloom (1956), Sanders (1966), Guszak (1967) and Barrett (1974); to information processing models of reading such as those developed by Chase and Clark (1972), Trabasso (1972) and Rumelhart (1976); to discourse analysis procedures such as to those described by Dawes (1966), Meyer (1975), Fredricksen (1972) and Kintsch (1974).

Taking as many variables into consideration as possible, we decided to use the framework of comprehension presented by Pearson and Johnson (1978) as the foundation for what would become the final framework for the analysis. It was selected because it is based upon rather recent research and theory development in psycholinguistics, cognitive psychology, computer science as well as "tried and true" practices in reading pedagogy. While their scheme is not a complete portrayal of comprehension tasks, as they readily acknowledge, it is a logically developed compilation of major comprehension tasks.

The Pearson and Johnson view of reading comprehension is best characterized by their phrase "comprehension is building bridges from the new to the known." In essence, one cannot learn anything unless it can be tied to something already known. Each individual possesses a vast storehouse of linguistic and experiential knowledge organized in networks of sometimes discrete but often overlapping categories. Borrowing terminology from computer scientists who specialize in the budding field of artificial intelligence, the categories within an individual's accumulated knowledge and experience are called *schemata* or *scripts*.

Comprehending written text involves developing linkages between the printed words, sentences, passages and their inter- and intra-relationships and the information already contained in the individual's scripts. Thus comprehension is highly active, not passive and it is probably true that readers bring more information to any printed page than they take from it. As passages are read, new information is assimilated into existing scripts; but at the same time that new information causes the scripts to be continually revised.

Pearson and Johnson present two major categories of comprehension tasks, word-level comprehension and proposition level comprehension. The nine word-level comprehension relations they have identified (synonymous, antonymous, associative, classificatory, analogous, connotative-denotative, multiple meaning, homographic and homophonous) will not be treated here because the purpose of the present chapter is to consider instruction in the comprehension of prose rather than concepts. We selected the remaining three categories of comprehension tasks and relations for inclusion in the framework for this analysis.

Propositions may be thought of as basic units of thought. They are what most of us know as dependent or independent clauses. "I went to the store." is a proposition and is also a sentence. The sentence, "I went to the store and applied for a job." has two propositions. Table 1 lists nine proposition level comprehension tasks, together with examples, where appropriate, and descriptions.

All nine proposition level tasks shown in Table 1 apply

equally well to comprehension of paragraphs, passages, and even longer units of discourse as they do to written materials of sentence and proposition length. Of these tasks, the ninth, Anaphora, deserves special attention because of its frequent usage in written discourse. Anaphora means, simply, the use of a word or words as a substitute for a preceding (or following) word or group of words. Anaphoric relations can be extremely difficult to process and research has shown (Richek, 1977; Dahlberg, 1978) that accuracy in assigning antecedents to anaphora is a crucial element of reading comprehension. Table 2 presents eight types of anaphoric relations, examples of each, and possible comprehension probes.

In addition to the nine items presented in Table 1, eight other tasks drawn from a variety of sources were also included in the final criterion frame. These eight additional comprehension tasks are:

1. Discerning fact and opinion
2. Evaluating bias in writing
3. Analyzing the author's purpose, style and effectiveness, i.e., the author's craft
4. Forming mental images while reading
5. Using reading-study skills such as dealing with graphs, maps, and other visual displays
6. Distinguishing reality from fantasy
7. *Reading* punctuation marks
8. Becoming familiar with a variety of tasks which might fall under the large catch-all umbrella called *literary form*. Included within literary form are such things as noting the plot, mood, setting, and climax of stories, and reading different types of writing including plays, poetry, nonfiction, biographies, descriptive, persuasive, and expository works.

In the analyses of materials and textbook chapters which follow, we will compare what is being taught or recommended against this rather straightforward set of tasks which is, in summary:

Table 1

Proposition Level Comprehension Tasks
As Proposed by Pearson and Johnson (1978, pp. 84-85)

Task	Example	Description
1. Paraphrase	The lady shut the door = The door was closed by the woman.	Recognizes the equivalence in meaning between two or more sentences.
2. Association		Student reads paragraph. Selects the one sentence that is out of place in the paragraph.
3. Main Idea—Details		Student reads paragraph. Then 1. Selects the main idea, *or* 2. Selects details that support a main idea.
4. Comparison	One paragraph is about bicycles, a second about canoes. Question: How are the pedals on a bicycle like the oars in a canoe?	After reading a paragraph, student compares relationships therein to relationships in another paragraph, story, or experience.
5. Figurative Language	1. John is a veritable gazelle = John can run fast.	1. Recognizes the equivalence between a figurative and a literal statement, *and* 2. Recognizes the difference in tone and feeling communicated by the two sentences.

6. Ambiguous Statements	Flying planes can be dangerous = 1. It can be dangerous to fly planes. 2. It can be dangerous to be around where airplanes are flying.	1. Recognizes that a single sentence can have more than one meaning, *and* 2. Selects the appropriate meaning for a given paragraph context.
7. Causal Relations	The people revolted because the new king was a tyrant. 1. Why did the people revolt? 2. What happened because the new king was a tyrant?	1. Can identify causes or explanations (answer *why* questions) *or* 2. Can identify effects (answer *what happened because* or *what will happen next* questions).
8. Sequence	John went into the store. He bought a new tire. Then he went home to put it on his bike. What happened after John bought a new tire?	After reading a paragraph, 1. Places events in the sequence explicated in the paragraph, *or* 2. Answers *when* or *what happened after* or *what happened before* questions.
9. Anaphora	*John* is my friend. *He* is kind. I *play ball. So does* Henry.	Recognizes the logical equivalence between an anaphoric (substitute) term and its antecedent.

Table 2

Anaphoric Relations

As Proposed by Pearson and Johnson (1978, pp. 124–125)

Relation	Example	Possible Comprehension Probe
1. Pronouns: I, me, we, us, you, he, him, they, them.	Mary has a friend named John. *She* picks *him* up on the way to school. *They* walk home together too.	Who gets picked up? Who picks him up? Name the person who gets picked up.
2. Locative (location) pronouns: here, there.	The team climbed to the top of Mt. Everest. Only a few people have been *there*.	Where have only a few people been? Name the place where only a few people have been.
3. Deleted nouns: usually an adjective serves as the anaphora.	The students scheduled a meeting but only a *few* attended. Apparently *several* went to the beach. *Others* attended a dance in the gym. *Only the most serious* actually came to the meeting. (Notice that each adjective phrase or adjective refers to students.)	Who went to the beach? Who attended the dance in our gym? What does the word *others* refer to?
4. Arithmetic Anaphora.	Mary and John entered the building. The *former* is tall and lovely. The *latter* is short and squatty. The *two* make an interesting couple.	Who is tall and lovely? Who makes an interesting couple?

78

| 5. Class inclusive anaphora: a superordinate word, substitutes for another word. | 1. The dog barked a lot. The *animal* must have seen a prowler.
2. The lion entered the clearing. The *big cat* looked graceful as it surveyed its domain.
3. John was awakened by a siren. He thought the *noise* would never stop. | 1. What animal must have seen a prowler? What does the word *animal* refer to?
2. What cat looked graceful? What does the word *cat* refer to?
3. What noise did John think would never stop? |
| 6. Inclusive Anaphora: that, this, the idea, the problem, these reasons. Can refer back to an entire phrase, clause, or passage. | 1. (After twenty pages discussing the causes of the Civil War.) For *these reasons*, the South seceded from the Union.
2. Someone was pounding on the door. *This* (or *it*) surprised Mary.
3. Crime is getting serious in Culver. The police have to do a better job with *this problem*.
4. "Do unto others as you would have them do unto you." *Such an idea* has been the basis of Christian theology for 2000 years. | 1. Why did the South secede from the Union?
2. What surprised Mary?
3. What do the police have to do a better job with?
4. What has been the basis of Christian theology for 2000 years? |

Table 2 - continued
Anaphoric Relations

7. Deleted predicate adjective: so is, is not, is too (also), *as is*	1. John is dependable. *So is* Henry. 2. John is dependable. Susan *is not.* 3. The lion was large but graceful. The tiger *was too.* 4. The lion, *as is* the tiger, is large but graceful.	1. Is Henry dependable? 2. Is Susan dependable? 3. Describe the tiger. 4. Describe the tiger.
8. Pro-verbs; *so does, can will,* have, and so on (or), can, does, will *too* (or), can, does, will *not,* *as did,* can will.	1. John went to school. *So did* Susan. 2. John went to school. Susan *did too.* 3. Henry will get an A. *So will* Theresa. 4. Amy can do a cartwheel. Matthew *cannot.* 5. Mom likes bologna. Dad *does not.* 6. John likes, *as does* Henry, potato chips.	1. What did Susan do? 2. What did Susan do too? 3. What will Theresa do? 4. Can Matthew do a cartwheel? What can't Matthew do? 5. Does Dad like bologna? 6. What does Henry like? Does Henry like potato chips?

17 Criterion Comprehension Tasks

1. Paraphrase
2. Association
3. Main Idea - Details
4. Comparison
5. Figurative Language
6. Ambiguous Statements
7. Causal Relations
8. Sequence
9. Anaphora
10. Fact and Opinion
11. Bias
12. Author's Craft
13. Mental Images
14. Study Skills
15. Reality and Fantasy
16. Punctuation
17. Literary Form

The above list would seem to have a very serious omission —Making Inferences. Obviously, inferences are an inevitable part of the comprehension process and comprehension of even the simplest prose passage requires a considerable quantity of inference making. Inferences are not listed separately because they are an inherent aspect of all eleven of the above tasks, *depending upon what information is explicitly or implicitly stated in the passage and what is derived from the reader's experience (script).* Depending on the nature of the question-answer relationship, comprehension is either textually explicit (a question has an obvious answer right on the page), textually implicit (an answer to a question can be inferred from information on the page), or scriptually implicit (there is no way to answer the question based on the information presented; prior knowledge and experience must be drawn upon). The following paragraph and the three questions which follow exemplify this:

> The center made the hook shot. The home crowd cheered with happiness and relief.
> 1. Who made the hook shot? (Textually explicit)
> 2. Whose team was the center on? (Textually implicit)
> 3. How many points for that basket? (Scriptally implicit)

In short, inference is not specifically presented in the framework because it can be and very often is involved in all of the seventeen tasks listed.

Basal Reading Materials

Reading materials at grade levels three and five from four major basal publishers* were analyzed (Ginn, 1976; Holt, Rinehart and Winston, 1977; Macmillan, 1975; Scott, Foresman, 1978). For each of these series we examined the scope and sequence charts and teacher manuals for all grade three and grade five materials to determine which comprehension tasks were included. We made no attempt to determine the extent or quality of instruction or to see if a given task was introduced,

Table 3
Grade Three Comprehension Tasks, Literal
and Inferential, in Four Basal Reading Series

GRADE 3								
Comprehension Tasks	Ginn		Holt, Rinehart and Winston		Macmillan		Scott, Foresman	
	L	I	L	I	L	I	L	I
1. Paraphrase			X					
2. Association								
3. Main Idea - Details (traits)	X	X	X	X	X		X	X
4. Comparison	X		X	X			X	
5. Figurative Language	X		X	X			X	
6. Ambiguous Statements			X					
7. Causal Relations		X		X		X	X	X
8. Sequence	X	X	X	X	X	X	X	
9. Anaphora							X	
10. Fact and Opinion		X	X				X	
11. Bias			X				X	
12. Author's Craft (purpose, style)	X	X	X	X	X		X	
13. Imagery								
14. Study Skills	X		X		X		X	
15. Fantasy - Reality			X			X		
16. Punctuation							X	
17. Literary Form	X	X	X	X			X	

* See list of basal materials at the end of this chapter.

maintained, or reinforced in the materials. Such detailed analysis was beyond the scope of this paper.

The analysis presented in Tables 3 and 4 is subject to several kinds of limitations. First, some tasks may indeed be taught or reinforced but are not included in scope and sequence charts. Second, some entries may receive only superficial attention while others are treated in-depth within the series. Third, authors and publishers sometimes use different terms to refer to the same tasks (e.g., title, main idea, plot, central thought, topic). Thus the present writers had to use their best

Table 4
Grade Five Comprehension Tasks, Literal
and Inferential, in Four Basal Reading Series

GRADE 5								
	Ginn		Holt, Rinehart and Winston		Macmillan		Scott, Foresman	
Comprehension Tasks	L	I	L	I	L	I	L	I
1. Paraphrase					X	X		
2. Association								
3. Main Idea - Details (traits)	X	X	X	X	X		X	
4. Comparison		X	X		X	X	X	
5. Figurative Language				X				X
6. Ambiguous Statements			X					X
7. Causal Relations		X	X	X	X	X	X	X
8. Sequence	X	X	X	X	X		X	
9. Anaphora							X	
10. Fact and Opinion	X	X	X	X	X	X	X	X
11. Bias			X		X		X	
12. Author's Craft (purpose, style)	X	X	X	X	X	X	X	
13. Imagery			X					
14. Study Skills	X		X		X		X	
15. Fantasy - Reality			X				X	
16. Punctuation			X				X	
17. Literary Form		X	X		X		X	

judgment in classifying some of the entries listed in the scope and sequence charts. For example, predicting outcomes may be thought of as forward inferencing or future causality while drawing conclusions about the reasons for some action or event might be viewed as backward inferencing. Both predicting outcomes and drawing conclusions, then, were viewed as inferential causal relation tasks. A second example is that character trait identifications were classified under details while character comparison tasks were placed under comparison. With these kinds of limitations in mind, Table 3 and Table 4 indicate which comprehension tasks were identified as being developed in the grades three and five materials.

Each table lists the seventeen comprehension tasks from the previously developed framework. Beneath each publisher is a *literal* and an *inferential* column. The check marks indicate whether a comprehension task is taught, and whether it is taught at a literal (textually explicit) or inferential (textually or scriptually implicit) level.

An examination of the tables reveals the following

1. At both grades in all or nearly all of the programs examined, comprehension instruction of the following tasks at both literal and inferential levels seems valued:
   a. Main Idea and Details
   b. Comparisons
   c. Causal Relations
   d. Sequence
   e. Fact and Opinion
   f. The Author's Craft
   g. Study Skills
   h. Literary Form
2. Little attention seemed to be given to:
   a. Paraphrase Tasks
   b. Association Tasks
   c. Figurative Language Comprehension
   d. Ambiguous Statement Comprehension
3. Practically no instruction at either grade level in the four series was provided in:

a. Using mental imagery
b. Reading punctuation marks
c. Dealing with anaphoric relations

One series included imagery in grade five, two included punctuation, and one taught anaphora (specified as pronoun referents) in grades three and five.

There are several reasons why comprehension tasks associated with paraphrasing, associating, figurative language, ambiguous statements, imagery, punctuation and anaphora appeared to receive little or no attention in the programs analyzed: 1) such tasks were presented in the programs but were not discerned in the scope and sequence charts; 2) the tasks were taught at levels of the programs not examined; 3) the tasks were deemed of lesser importance by the authors of the programs than the ones included.

Professional Textbooks

While the instructional programs teachers use probably have the greatest influence on the comprehension tasks they teach and the instructional strategies they use, other likely influences are the professional textbooks they read in undergraduate or graduate courses. We, therefore, felt it would be of value to examine a selected sample of recent professional textbooks to determine the comprehension tasks that such sources were emphasizing.

Since nearly 100 textbooks intended for undergraduates and graduate reading courses are in print, certain criteria were used to select the final sample of textbooks analyzed. Arbitrarily, any book not published within the past five years was not considered. A large number of books published since 1974 were ruled out because they either contained no discrete chapter on reading comprehension, or because within a discrete chapter they contained no listing of comprehension tasks. They taught "how" but not "what." All books examined included various instructional strategies that teachers might use and some of those suggestions are described toward the end of this chapter. Of the dozen or more reading books published since

1974 which contain discrete chapters on comprehension with full discussions of reading tasks, five were selected for inclusion here. Though their overlap is inevitable (and even desirable), they were selected because they were sufficiently different in content, organization, or extent.

Hittleman, in *Developmental Reading: A Psycholinguistic Perspective* (1978), presents 14 specific tasks to facilitate pupils' understanding of sentences. Most of his tasks are equally applicable to paragraphs and longer prose passages.

1. Recognizing "who" or "what" the sentence is about.
   Felice got into the blue truck.

2. Recognizing "what is being done" by the "who" or "what" of the sentence.
   Raymond *hugged his aunt and uncle.*

3. Recognizing and using the signals for information that indicates "where" something is or is done. The signals for "where" information are *under, cover, in, on, at, to, between, among, behind, in front of, through.*
   The class had its morning recess *in the school gym.*

4. Recognizing and using the signals for information that indicates "when" something is done or happens. The signals for "when" information are *before, after, later, while, as, now, then.*
   Frank was able to get inside his house *before the thunder and lightning started.*

5. Recognizing and using the signals for information that indicates "how" something is done. The signals for "how" information are the adverbial endings *-ly, like, as.*
   They walked *quietly* up the steps.

6. Recognizing and using the signals for information that indicates "how long" or "how much" something is. The signals for "how long" and "how much" information are *for, about, almost, as long (much) as, until* (and information dealing with any sort of measurement).
   The cat sat *for hours* waiting for the canary to leave its cage.

7. Recognizing and using the signals for information that indicates a "condition" exists. The signals for "condition" information are *is, seems, appears.*
   Harry *is* the name of my pet cat.

8. Recognizing and using information that indicates "what kind of" thing something is. The clues for "what kind of" information are the possible transforms of the "condition" sentences.

 > The *tired* quarterback looked at the clock and wished the game was over. (The quarterback is tired.)

9. Understanding how some information in a sentence can be moved without changing the meaning of the sentence.

 > The architect skillfully drew the lines of the house.

 > Skillfully, the architect drew the lines of the house.

10. Understanding that different sentences can have practically the same meaning.

 > Sandra painted the furniture to match the drapes her mother made.

 > The furniture was painted by Sandra to match the drapes made by her mother.

11. Recognizing and using the signals for information that indicates certain information about someone or something has been placed within the sentence. The clues to this extra, descriptive information are *who, which,* and *that.*

 > The test questions, *which* seemed unanswerable by all the students, covered everything *that* they had learned about the geography of Asia.

12. Recognizing and using the signals for information that indicates certain information has been replaced. The clues to the replaced information are *I, you, he, she, it, they, we, us, them, their, his, her, your, our, him, this, these.*

 > "Wait until you see *this*," shouted Randy, running to the other kids with *his* stamp collection.

13. Understanding that words are often left out of a sentence and that the reader has to mentally replace the omitted information. The clue that information has been omitted is that questions beginning with *what* or *did what* can be asked at the point the information was omitted.

 > While everybody was eating the hot pancakes, Leslie made some more. (More *what*?)

14. Understanding how different sentences can be connected together, and conversely, how sentences can be separated into other sentences. The signals to understanding the connecting of sentences are a variety of conjunctions that seem to signal four types of relationships (Hittleman, 1978, pp. 237–240).

To these tasks, Hittleman adds six paragraph patterns (enumeration, generalization, comparison/contrast, sequence, effect/

cause, and question/answer) and, within longer discourse, seven paragraph functions (introductory, explanatory, narrative, descriptive, definitional, transitional, and concluding).

In *Reading-Language Instruction: Innovative Practices,* Ruddell (1974) identifies three levels of comprehension and shows the relationship among these three levels and seven types of what he refers to as comprehension skill competencies.

	Comprehension Levels		
Skill Competencies	Factual	Interpretive	Applicative
1. Details			
a. Identifying	X	X	
b. Comparing	X	X	X
c. Classifying		X	X
2. Sequence	X	X	X
3. Cause and Effect	X	X	X
4. Main Idea	X	X	X
5. Predicting Outcome		X	X
6. Valuing			
a. Personal judgment	X	X	X
b. Character trait identification	X	X	X
c. Author's motive identification		X	X
7. Problem Solving			X

(Ruddell, 1974, p. 380)

Lapp and Flood report in *Teaching Reading to Every Child* a list of eleven types of conditions which require inferential processing in reading. Though the list by no means is presented as being complete, it is a good representation of tasks with which readers need to deal.

Type	Example
1. Ambiguity in sentences and clauses.	Flying planes can be dangerous. I like her cooking. She fed her dog biscuits.
2. Unclear anaphoric referents.	Zoe and Zeke were masons. They were paid by Vera and Velma. *They* were inflexible.
3. Unclear cataphoric referents.	It was a day in spring. The month when Jim lost his job.
4. Unclear deictic referents (person, place, time).	Paula and Patrick were meeting in the afternoon for food. Patrick was so late that Paula left.
5. Unclear topical referents.	It was always this way. They had so much fun when they went there that they decided to return again.
6. Partial lexicalization.	The set disappeared.
7. Missing connective.	Tony drove too fast. The police didn't care about the emergency.
8. Unclear segmentation.	Maria went to the fire station. Bernard and Maria lived happily ever after. They got the firemen to help them put out the fire.
9. Need for reduction.	Tom was whining, coughing, vomiting, crying, tossing.
10. Need for extensions	Emma lost her tooth. Her father put her quarter in her piggy bank.
11. Pragmatic considerations.	The house was 80 years old and the *crew* arrive.

(Lapp and Flood, 1978, p. 302)

In their book, *Focused Reading Instruction* (1974), Otto, Chester, McNeil and Meyers state, "We are convinced that in order to get down to the business of *individualization* and *accountability*—two of the main challenges that face us in reading education—we must be able to *focus* on teaching. . . . Focusing instruction through the use of objectives and objective based teaching" (ix). From this point of view about reading, they present an outline of comprehension tasks at six levels intended to span the elementary grades.

Level A
1. Identifies a topic: pictures
2. Determines sequence: first or last event
3. Uses logical reasoning: synthesizes information
4. Uses logical reasoning: predicts outcomes

Level B
1. Identifies a topic: paragraphs
2. Determines sequence: event before and after
3. Uses logical reasoning: synthesizes information
4. Uses logical reasoning: predicts outcomes
5. Reads for details

Level C
1. Identifies a topic: paragraphs
2. Determines sequence: event before and after
3. Uses logical reasoning: determines cause-effect relationships
4. Reads for details

Level D
1. Identifies a topic sentence
2. Determines sequence: explicit and implicit relationships
3. Uses logical reasoning: determines cause-effect relationships
4. Uses logical reasoning: reasons from a premise
5. Reads for details: interprets negative sentences
6. Reads for details: interprets sentences with right-branching
7. Reads for details: interprets sentences written in passive voice
8. Uses context clues: unfamiliar words

Level E
1. Identifies a main idea: paragraphs
2. Determines sequence: implicit relationships
3. Uses logical reasoning: reasons syllogistically
4. Uses logical reasoning: reasons inductively
5. Reads for details: interprets sentences with one centrally embedded part
6. Reads for details: interprets negative passive sentences
7. Uses context clues: unfamiliar words
8. Determines the meaning of prefixes

Level F
1. Identifies a main idea: two paragraphs
2. Determines sequence: orders events along a time line
3. Uses logical reasoning: applies a premise
4. Reads for details: interprets sentences with one centrally embedded part combined with right-branching
5. Uses context clues: unfamiliar words
6. Determines the meaning of suffixes

Level G
1. Identifies a main-idea statement: extended passage

2. Determines sequential relationships between events from separate passages
3. Uses logical reasoning: reasons syllogistically
4. Uses logical reasoning: applies a premise
5. Uses context clues: obscure meaning of familiar words
6. Determines the meaning of prefixes

(Otto, Chester, McNeil and Meyers, 1974, pp. 184–185)

To this listing they add a number of other related, though not so measurable, objectives under the categories of self-directed, interpretive, and creative reading.

Guszak identifies five major categories of comprehension tasks in "Reading: Comprehension Skills," *Reading: Foundations and Instructional Strategies* (Lamb & Arnold, 1976). Beneath each category, as shown in Table 5, are listed several specific subskills.

When comparing the comprehension tasks listed in these five reading textbooks with the 17 criterion comprehension tasks described earlier in this chapter, a good deal of overlap is apparent. All but the Lapp/Flood list make reference (though sometimes using different terms) to main idea/details, sequence and causal relations. Several cite comparison tasks, and making judgments. Two lists each refer to paraphrasing and processing anaphoric relations. One lists sentence ambiguity. All five textbooks include sections on study skills and four of them describe tasks associated with matters of literary form and aspects of the authors craft.

Summary of the Comprehension Tasks Presented in
Four Basal Readers and Five Professional Reading Textbooks

Table 6 presents three clusters of comprehension tasks. The first set includes those tasks which are widely taught (according to the Basal Series examination) and widely advocated (according to the Professional Reading Textbook examination). The second set includes those less in common practice, and the third set includes those which were rarely or never mentioned.

Table 5
Reading Skills Checklist: Comprehension
As Proposed by Guszak in Lamb and Arnold (1976, p. 378)

Predicting/Extending	Locating Information	Remembering	Organizing	Evaluating Critically
Predicts convergent outcomes from: picture and title title oral description story situations	Locates specifics within written materials phrase(s) sentence(s) paragraph(s) page numbers parts of a story (beginning, middle, end, etc.)	Remembering simple sentence content Remembering the content of two or more simple sentences and sentence sets	Retells: sentence sentence set paragraph story Outlines orally the sequence of the story	Makes judgments about the desirability of a: character situation Makes judgments about the validity of a: story description argument, etc. by making both external and internal comparison
Predicts divergent outcomes	Locating information with book parts titles stories table of contents	Remembering paragraph content Remembering story content	Reorganizes a communication into a: cartoon picture picture sequence	Making judgments about whether stories are fictional or nonfictional by noting: reality fantasy exaggeration
Explain story character actions Explain gadget operations Generalizes from sets of information in story(ies) (include task of identifying an unstated main idea).	Locating information with reference aids picture dictionaries maps (political) dictionaries encyclopedias atlases globes telephone books newspapers			Making judgments about whether the author is trying to amuse, bias, etc. the reader
Restores omitted words in context				Detects in reading materials the following propaganda techniques: —bad names, e.g. wallflower —glad names, e.g. superstar
Labels feelings of characters, i.e. sad - glad				
Explains why story characters hold certain viewpoints				

Table 6

Comprehension Tasks

Rated by Frequency of Mention in Four Basal Series and Five Professional
Reading Textbooks

Most Taught or Recommended	1. Main Ideas and Supporting Details 2. Sequence 3. Causal Relations 4. Facts and Opinions 5. Reality and Fantasy 6. Comparisons 7. Study Skills 8. Literary Form 9. The Author's Craft
Sometimes Taught or Recommended	1. Associations 2. Detecting Bias
Least Taught or Recommended	1. Anaphoric Relations 2. Paraphrasing 3. Mental Imagery 4. Punctuation 5. Figurative Language 6. Ambiguous Statements

The comprehension tasks in the top set probably came as a surprise to no one. They are common tasks which have long been taught. It is somewhat surprising that detecting bias fell in the middle category since it is such an important type of critical reacting. Associations (discerning and discarding irrelevant information) is either not taught too frequently or it is hidden beneath other labels. The bottom category holds several surprises. Paraphrasing sentences and paragraphs, and processing figurative language, ambiguous statements and anaphoric relations would seem to be vitally important comprehension tasks deserving more attention than they seem to be getting. The remaining two tasks, forming mental images while reading, and *reading* (not writing) punctuation marks received minimal mention and, thus, are probably rarely taught.

In the remaining pages of this chapter attention will be shifted from tasks suggested by current professional and instructional sources for children which are expected to facilitate their comprehension of prose passages to instructional strategies for teachers when they teach reading comprehension.

Instructional Strategies

The current literature related to reading instruction shows an increased concern for the teaching of comprehension. For example, recent books by Smith (1975), Gerhard (1975), Griese (1977), and Pearson and Johnson (1978) are devoted entirely to aspects of teaching reading comprehension or comprehension in general. It is not our purpose here to present an analysis of the strategies for teaching comprehension of prose passages contained in such sources. Rather the intent is to highlight what we perceive as the current status of selected teaching strategies designed to facilitate student comprehension of prose passages.

For many years the standard approach to teaching the comprehension of prose passages was certain strategies:

1. Relate the content of the passage to the reader's background.
2. Introduce vocabulary which may prove troublesome.
3. Set purposes or prose questions to guide the reader.
4. Have the readers read the passage part by part or in total.
5. Determine how well the readers have understood the passage by asking questions related to the purposes or questions introduced before reading.
6. Reread the passage, or parts thereof, to verify understanding or for new purposes.

This approach, or modest variations of it, is still recommended in instructional and professional sources. And it would appear to have merit if teachers use it selectively, judiciously, and creatively with the intention of helping students transfer some of its strategies to their personal reading.

Johnson and Barrett

On the other hand, if teachers carry out the strategies in the approach in a perfunctory manner, certain unfortunate tendencies can result on the part of teachers and students alike. First, there may be a tendency on the part of teachers to deemphasize the importance of relating student language and experiential background to the forthcoming passage. Thus, students may not become actively involved in "building bridges from the known to the new." Second, the perfunctory setting of purposes and questions before reading may lead to a tendency on the part of teachers to focus on bits of literal information, since these are the easiest types of questions to develop. This tendency in turn may condition students to pass over incidental information when they read which might contribute significantly to their understanding. Third, students may develop a tendency to become passive rather than active readers, if the approach is implemented in a "cookbook fashion." In other words, they may become conditioned to thinking comprehension of a passage is a mundane exercise requiring minimal cognitive involvement on their part.

The concerns raised about the perfunctory implementation of the standard approach for teaching the comprehension of prose passages provide a point of departure for presenting further comments about three of the strategies included in the approach, namely: 1) relating the reader's background to the content of the passage; 2) setting purposes for reading the passage; 3) asking questions before, during, and after reading.

Background of the reader. As implied in our brief discussion of the standard teaching approach, the importance of the background of the reader has been recognized by practitioners for years. It is not a new idea. What is new in our opinion is that the relatively recent work of theoreticians and researchers who have been interested in this variable and its influence on comprehension has influenced authors of instructional and professional materials to give increased attention to strategies which help readers relate their storehouses of language, knowledge, and experiences—their scripts or schemata—to the content of prose passages.

To illustrate the latter point, consider that reading comprehension has been described by certain contemporary authors as relating new experiences to the already known (Smith, 1975), building bridges from the new to the known (Pearson & Johnson, 1978), and reconstructing the author's message (Goodman & Goodman, 1977). Each of these descriptions suggests, either implicitly or explicitly, that comprehension depends upon what the reader brings to a passage. Moreover, these authors are familiar to reading educators and do through their writings influence, directly or indirectly, the strategies used by teachers in the classroom.

A specific example of a current teaching strategy that recognizes the influence of the reader's background on comprehension is the advanced organizer. An advanced organizer is a statement used to ready the reader to comprehend a passage to be read. Ausubel (1963), the originator of this strategy, suggested that its purpose is to relate the materials to be comprehended to the readers cognitive structure. In other words, an advanced organizer is to call attention to what a reader already knows about the content of a given passage as well as to what is new. Ausubel did point out, however, that the efficacy of this strategy to facilitate comprehension was proportionate to the degree of interface between the cognitive structure of the reader and the new information to be assimilated. The research dealing with advanced organizers, which is reviewed in other chapters in this volume, bears out this complexity and others. Nevertheless, the use of advanced organizers as a classroom strategy has made headway because of their potential to facilitate the cognitive interaction of readers with an author's message, thus enhancing the possibility of comprehension.

Purposes for reading. As pointed out in the discussion of the standard instructional strategy for teaching comprehension of prose passages, purposes for reading are often determined and initiated by the teacher. Stauffer (1975) has argued against this practice for years. His directed-reading-thinking activity [in which the student's role in reading passages is to *predict* (set purposes) *read* (process ideas) and *prove* (test answers) and the teacher's role is to activate and agitate thought by asking such questions as What do you think? and Why you think so? and to require evidence] removes this responsibility from the teacher and places it with the reader. He argues that the reading-thinking process must begin with the reader. Readers must be active. They must conjecture or develop questions about what the passage holds on the basis of information available. These self-initiated predictions or questions then become the students' purposes for reading. The teacher's job is to keep the process active and alive.

Many of Stauffer's ideas are supported currently by such people as Smith (1975), and Goodman & Goodman (1977), and Hittleman (1978). For example, the idea that the comprehension of prose passages can be facilitated if readers are taught to use strategies in which they continually predict and prove as they process print is a very current theme. It suggests that instructional strategies used by teachers should involve students in setting their purposes for reading so that they will feel responsible for and actively involved in achieving such purposes.

One task that is commonly used for developing the strategy of predicting and proving is the cloze procedure. Cloze passages designed to teach this strategy need not have every fifth word deleted. Rather they may have every seventh or tenth word deleted or every noun or verb or adjective deleted. Exact replication of the author's words is not required either when cloze passages are used for this type of instruction; synonyms are accepted. The point is that cloze tasks focus on what the reader knows in anticipation of the message the author intended. Cloze tasks, then, can contribute to the acquisition of the strategy of predicting and proving and are being used by classroom teachers for this purpose.

Questioning

Since the publication of Bloom's *Taxonomy of Educational Objectives* (1956), a number of reading theoreticians and educators have proposed taxonomies of reading comprehension (not necessarily heirarchial) which provide frameworks for asking questions (Barrett, 1974; Guszak, 1976; Sanders, 1966).

Recently Lapp and Flood (1978) combined and summarized these taxonomies of question types in relation to the six cognitive levels of Bloom's taxonomy: knowledge, comprehension, application, analysis, synthesis and evaluation.

Levels of Cognitive Development	Reading Comprehension
	Text Explicit Information
Knowledge (recall)	*(literal comprehension)*
	Identification of sounds letters phrases sentences paragraphs
	Recognition and recall of details main ideas sequence comparison cause-and-effect relationships character traits patterns
Comprehension (understanding)	Translation of ideas or information explicitly stated classifying generalizing outlining summarizing synthesizing
Application (abstracting)	*Text Implicit Information*
	(inferential comprehension)
	Realization of one's experiences and textual exposures
	Inferring details main ideas sequence comparisons cause-and-effect relationships character traits
Analysis (analyzing)	Predicting outcomes

Synthesis
(production)

Interpreting figurative language
imagery, character, motives, and
responses

Synthesizing
convergently
divergently

World Knowledge Information

Evaluation
(judging)

(critical comprehension)

Making evaluative judgments of
reality or fantasy
fact or opinion
adequacy and validity
appropriateness
worth, desirability, and
acceptability

Valuing
Propaganda detection
euphemism
fallacy of reasoning
statistical fallacy (maps, charts)
stereotyping
oversimplification

Appreciation

Emotional response to content
Identification with characters
or incidents
Reactions to the author's use
of language
Reactions to the author's
word pictures

(Lapp and Flood, 1978, pp. 297–298)

It is safe to say that a good deal of instructional time is spent in asking students questions – prior to reading, during reading, and after reading a selection. It follows that a lot of student time is spent answering questions, both those asked orally by one's self or the teacher, and those ubiquitous written questions found at the end of so many stories, chapters and books. One might legitimately ask whether asking questions really helps *develop* comprehension or if it merely *assesses* it. Questioning likely satisfies elements of both.

In Table 7, Singer (1978) presents an adaptation of Ruddell's discussion (1974) of question purposes (types) which provides a useful basis for considering the various roles which questions can play. He points out that teacher's questions, may be used to focus on an issue, extend the level of a discussion, or clarify a point, among other things. In turn various types of questions may require students to respond at the literal, interpretive, applied or evaluative levels. Singer's paradigm, then, provides a useful way of viewing teacher-student interaction when questioning by the teacher is involved.

Questions have been a standard instructional strategy in reading comprehension for decades. They serve a critical role in any discussion activity and are obviously useful for both informal and formal assessment.

Summary of instructional strategies. To reiterate, this section focused upon three elements in instructional strategies designed to facilitate comprehension of prose passages: 1) language and informational background of the reader; 2) purposes for reading; and 3) questioning before, during, and after reading. These elements, while not new, were highlighted because current thinking related to the teaching of reading comprehension supports their importance. Suffice it to say that professional and instructional materials are suggesting to teachers to place emphasis on these elements as they attempt to facilitate their students' efforts to comprehend prose passages.

A Final Note

The purpose of this chapter was to examine and analyze suggested instructional practices, designed to promote children's comprehension of prose practices, found in a selected sample of current professional and instructional sources dealing with the teaching of reading. Although a different sample of such sources may have produced somewhat different information, it seems reasonable to suggest that the instructional practices highlighted in the preceding pages are representative of those currently in use. It also appears that some of the current thinking about the comprehension of prose passages by theoreticians and researchers in the cognitive sciences has been translated into

Table 7
Teacher-Student Interaction
(Singer, 1978, p. 903)

Teacher-student
interaction

Who talks	*Function*
Teacher	Question
Student	Response

Questioning strategy

Type	*Purpose*	*Question*
Focusing	Initiate discussion or refocus on the issue.	What did you like best about the story? What was the question we started to answer?
Controlling	Direct or dominate the discussion.	First, would you review the plot?
Ignoring or rejecting	Maintain current trend in discussion. Disregard a student's interest.	Would you mind if we don't go into that now?
Extending	Obtain more information at a particular level of discussion.	What other information do we have about the hero?
Clarifying	Obtain a more adequate explanation. Draw out a student.	Would you explain what you mean?
Raising	Have discussion move from factual to interpretive, inferential, or abstraction and generalization level.	We now have enough examples. What do they have in common? (Abstract) Was it always true for his behavior? (Generalization)

Response Level

Factual or literal (What the author said)

Interpretive (Integration of ideas of inference)

Applied (Transfer of ideas or judgment that idea is subsumed under broader generalization)

Evaluative (Using cognitive or affective criteria for judging issue) instructional terms by the authors of recently published sources.

While many of the current practices are likely to persist, it is equally likely that, as a result of recent and present comprehension research, a chapter such as the present one, written a decade from now, might look substantially different. Comprehension has been and will be the most pervasive and intriguing aspect of reading acquisition.

Instructional Materials

AARON, IRA E., and SYLVIA CARTER. *Step Right Up!* Grade 3_2, Basics in Reading. Glenview, Illinois: Scott, Foresman, 1978.

CLYMER, THEODORE, and GLORIA L. HOORWORTH. *Inside Out.* Level 9, Ginn Reading 720 Program. Lexington, Massachusetts: Ginn, 1976.

CLYMER, THEODORE, BLAIR McCRACKEN, and CONSTANCE M. McCULLOUGH. *Measure Me Sky.* Level 12, Ginn Reading 720 Program. Lexington, Massachusetts: Ginn, 1976.

EVERTTS, ELDONNA L., and BERNARD J. WEISS. *Special Happenings.* Level 12, Holt Basic Reading System. New York: Holt, Rinehart and Winston, 1977.

SMITH, CARL B., RONALD WARDHAUGH, and JAMES DOUGLAS. *Good News.* Level 16, Series r, New Macmillan Reading Program. New York: Macmillan, 1975.

SMITH, CARL B., RONALD WARDHAUGH, and LARRY A. HARRIS. *Signals.* Level 27, Series r, New Macmillan Reading Program. New York: Macmillan, 1975.

SMITH, RICHARD G., and ROBERT TIERNEY. *Fins and Tails.* Grade 5, Basics in Reading. Glenview, Illinois: Scott, Foresman, 1978.

WEISS, BERNARD J. *Freedom's Ground.* Holt Basic Reading System, Level 14. New York: Holt, Rinehart and Winston, 1977.

Can We Integrate Research and Instruction on Reading Comprehension?

Thomas Trabasso
University of Chicago

When I was asked to read, review, and discuss the respective papers by Baker and Stein, Levin and Pressley, and Johnson and Barrett, I was told by the editors that I would be reading reviews focusing on three content areas. The first, by Baker and Stein, would review what we know about reading comprehension as a result of basic research on the problem. The second, by Levin and Pressley, would present and evaluate techniques used to teach reading comprehension. The third, by Johnson and Barrett, would be concerned with what was actually done to teach comprehension in classroom practice. The notions that one could compare what we know about comprehension from laboratory studies with how we use research to assess, teach, and improve comprehension and how instructional practice coincided with what we knew to be sound and proven procedure all appealed to me. Thus I approached the papers with anticipation and hope, assuming that there would be direct and mutual influences between the laboratory and the classroom. Upon reading the three reviews, I came away disappointed and even dismayed. In my discussion, I shall try to register the basis for some of my chagrin. In the hope that I can restore some of my original optimism, I shall try to make constructive comments or point

The writing of this paper was supported by National Institute of Education Grant NIE-G-77-0018 to Thomas Trabasso.

103

to instructional examples which appear to be based upon sound and proven practices which were not included in the reviews.

The central problem with the literature cited in the three reviews is the apparent lack of influence between the respective three domains. Baker and Stein focus primarily on studies of narrative or prose recall where the text materials are largely heard rather than read. Levin and Pressley discuss experiments which demonstrate some benefit for recall or question answering on ambiguous text which was preceded or accompanied by pictorial or single word context cues. Johnson and Barrett borrow a taxonomy of tasks from secondary sources on comprehension (Pearson & Johnson, 1978; Johnson & Pearson, 1978) to compare basal reader programs, finding that, unlike the emphasis upon recall studies by educational and developmental psychologists, the programs developed by publishers focus on tasks which ask the students to identify main ideas, learn temporal sequences, find causal relations, and learn facts. Strangely enough, Johnson and Barrett do not examine actual curricula or practice but rely upon commercial programs for what they think is actually taught. Nor do they evaluate what skills are most important to teach, which procedures are most effective, and what practical tasks actually capture the content which is summarized in their taxonomy. Their examples struck me as limited and laboratory rather than classroom based.

Let us first look at the Baker and Stein review. The most vivid impression is that reading comprehension, as studied by psychologists, is regarded as not different from memory for prose and it seemes to matter little whether the material is heard or read. Throughout both the Baker-Stein and Levin-Pressley papers, the nearly exclusive measure of comprehension is one of recall, mostly verbatim recall, although occasionally probed or recognition questions are used. Other memory measures such as verification or paraphrase or summarization are infrequent and almost no other product of comprehension is described, save some work on story production. The central working thesis must be, as Baker and Stein indicate, that that which is not well understood is also not well remembered.

The focus on memory and its measurement has historical precedent in psychology but its dominance in what is purported to be comprehension research strikes me as rather restrictive, especially when compared to what is done in practice (see Johnson & Barrett and below). While the use of memory tasks operationalizes comprehension (and we know that subjective judgments of comprehension are correlated with recall (Bransford & Johnson, 1973), they can produce misleading results. For example, even when children are assessed as to their "sensitivity" to "main ideas," we find that recall is the index of understanding. Unfortunately, as Baker and Stein note, since the purported main ideas are complete, concrete, surface sentences and non-main ideas are incomplete, more abstract, sentence fragments, then it is not surprising that main ideas are recalled better. The reason for superior recall, however, is less likely to be because of the central role that these sentences play in a narrative as it is to be because of completeness and the ease with which the child can understand and imagine the events portrayed. What are called main ideas are really sentences that are easier to commit to memory, independent of the text.

What is needed here is an a priori analytic or theoretical basis for deciding what is a main idea or at least specific criteria for such a decision. The theory should not only analyze text but include some consideration about how children process these main ideas and commit them to memory for later use in answering questions and solving problems.

One promising approach to identifying which elementary sentences, called propositions, are important to the cohesiveness of a text, and therefore important to the ease with which children can process text, is that of Kintsch and Vipond (in press). Kintsch and Vipond analyze a text into basic units called propositions. Propositions are essentially simple sentences which contain one predicate and one or more of its arguments. That is, a verb and its subject, object, instrument, or other case relations. These authors identify central or important propositions by which arguments are repeated frequently across propositions. As a result, sentences (propositions) are linked by common arguments and that proposition which contains the largest number of direct or indirect links becomes most central.

Kintsch and Vipond have also simulated which propositions get into memory by a computer model. The model is psychological in nature in that it includes parameters for the size of working space in memory and the number of propositions which can be taken into memory. These parameters are important since the model shows that text which is low in cohesiveness is not well understood (represented in memory) if the size of short term memory is limited. In addition, coherence as measured by their analysis was shown to be a better predictor of readability ratings, comprehension ratings as well as ease of recall and details of what content is recalled.

On the positive side, the Baker and Stein review takes what is another, almost dominant, view in comprehension research on adults. The dominant view goes under the heading of "schema theory" (Shank, 1977; Lehnert, 1977). The idea is that we have many stored experiences which guide our interpretation of new experiences or events. Stored experiences are abstracted and generalized from specific episodes and these scripts enable us to interpret events described in narratives, relate them to what we know, store the new knowledge (facts, opinions, events) with the old, and store this information in memory. Once stored, these facts may be used along with what is known to make inferences, answer questions, paraphrase, summarize, etc.

Story grammars are a part of this general schema theory and are used to describe the knowledge we have about narratives which allows us to interpret stories as to their content, the functions of sentences and their causal or temporal relations.

These grammars, serving as analytic devices for stories, could provide valuable insight into some of the factors which Johnson and Barrett list. For example, main ideas in stories should be those events which are causally related to the goals and purposes of the protagonist. Noncentral ideas would be those events which are not purposeful or related to the goals of the protagonist or which are not causally (logically or semantically) related to other sentences (see Omanson, 1978, for a detailed analysis of central events in narratives). Stein and Glenn

(1978) commented on this possibility. In addition, the causal-relations between sentences represent a special kind of knowledge which allows the child to set up expectations of events in narratives, to relate new information to other ideas expressed in the text or to what one already knows, and to create a coherent representation of the text in memory. Finally, the grammars point to the temporal sequence character of events. That is, in well-formed stories, events are ordered in time according to certain sequences of categories. Knowledge of the categories and their expected order helps the child to encode events in their proper or natural temporal order of occurrence. Note, therefore, that four of the comprehension tasks stressed by reading programs receive potential analytic treatment by the story grammar or schema or script approach: main ideas, sequence of events, causal relations, and facts (events *per se*).

In contrast, Levin and Pressley are vague about what they mean by activation of knowledge and how this knowledge is actually used in comprehension. The story grammars and schema theory indicate one kind of knowledge that is important and which can be activated not just by the teacher but by the text itself through the use of well-formed narratives or content which is script-like, that is, highly familiar to the child. This activation of knowledge is common classroom procedure. In the readiness stage of reading, the teacher discusses with the children those experiences and concepts which are relevant to the content. If the child does not know the concept, it is taught. Apparently such instruction is content oriented. In contrast, the scripts, schemata, and story grammars are general, higher-order organizations of ideas and do not specify content. Rather, they are abstractions or categorizations of the content organized according to well-known situations or regularly occurring aspects of narratives.

Questions arise with respect to the review of Levin and Pressley: What is activated by single word concepts or pictures and why does this activation facilitate comprehension? Presumably the picture includes familiar objects or activities which are externally organized. The possibility exists that the facilitation observed results from information in pictures which is stored in memory independent of the information in the text. The facilitation of recall could result from recall of picture content *per se* and not recall or comprehension of the text. What is needed in this research is inclusion of control conditions where the children study picture contexts alone and then are asked the same probe questions. An additional factor is the organization contained in pictures *per se*. We could use analysis of both the structural relations within pictures and text as well as how pictures relate to text. Such analyses remain to be done.

The title of the Baker and Stein paper as well as the studies surveyed by Levin and Pressley promise to help us understand the development of comprehension and what strategies are characteristic of or appropriate for children at different levels of reading skill. One does not, however, learn about what is the development of comprehension, other than the recurrent finding that older children recall more or that some methods seem to work for older but not younger children. One problem is that what are called developmental studies are merely experiments done on children at different ages. Seldom is the study done on reading or with some measure of reading skill as a covariate. What is also missing are longitudinal studies on the same children as they progress from prereading stages to skilled reading stages. The lack of the latter doesn't disqualify age-related studies but it creates problems of not knowing what are the bases for age-related differences. What we seem to have before us is a list of ways in which younger children are less good at remembering oral prose. We would like to know why these so-called failures occur, independent of possible memory capacity differences. Since memory differences predominate between children of different ages, one wonders why these weren't controlled for, as in the Paris and Upton (1976) series. If one were to match a five year old with an eight year old on memory for information independent of the content in question, would there still be differences in their ability to answer inferential questions? If one were to query children of different ages on content or relations between events as they were heard or read and if one matched children of different ages on their understanding of these on-line events, would they differ in subsequent recall? If older children do better on inference questions than younger ones, when memory for premises is controlled, then we would have evidence that older children can infer or relate events better than younger children, independent of memory. This is, in fact, what Paris & Upton (1976) and Omanson, Warren, and Trabasso (in press) have found.

In their discussion of questioning, Johnson and Barrett raise an interesting issue by asking whether questions help develop comprehension or merely assess it. Suppose we assume that the child tries to interpret a narrative by finding the logical and causal relations between events, as assumed by general schema theory. We might futher suppose that the asking of causal questions (i.e., ones involving why? what happened? how?) may promote comprehension because they promote or force the child to find connections between events which he or she may not find otherwise. Alternatively, on the other side of the issue, those children who can find such relations are those who understand the text better and also show better recall. Wimmer (1979) has done a clever comparison of kinds of questions during listening to a story on recall. Wimmer read to children, four to eight years of age, the farmer and the donkey story which involves a large number of embedded episodes where the farmer asks other animals to help him get the donkey into the barn. Wimmer asked one group of children why? questions on each action, and thereby required an answer involving a preceding sentence. He asked a second group of who? or whom? questions where the content of the questions was within a sentence. He found no effect of which question was asked on recall but he did find a higher correlation between performance on why questions and recall than he found between performance on the who/whom questions and recall. These data favor the assessment over the promotion argument on questions. One possible artifact in Wimmer's study is the restriction or range of scores in the who/whom question condition—that is, the high rate of performance reduces variance and the degree of correlation.

Wimmer's study suggests that knowledge and not strategies or "metacognition" may be more important in comprehension.

Baker and Stein's apparent commitment to metacognition

(Flavell & Wellman, 1977), to account for age-related differences in recall and presumably comprehension, contrasts sharply with the results of Chi's experiments (1978). Children who know more about a subject such as chess or dinosaur names actually recall more than less sophisticated adults, despite reasonable assumptions that adults are more cognizant of their abilities and more strategic in their learning approaches. Perhaps Levin and Pressley's as well as Johnson and Barrett's emphasis on prior knowledge and its activation in teaching (what the reader already knows prior to reading) is well taken, given Wimmer and Chi's results.

Baker and Stein as well as Levin and Pressley frequently cite the contribution of the text *per se* to comprehension. Text factors seem to be omitted from Johnson and Barrett's review. But, we may ask, what is a text? What role does it play? What kind of structures, other than well- or ill-formed stories, promote comprehension? How do we measure cohesiveness of text? Levin and Pressley's use of pictures or concepts as context in understanding degraded or ambiguous texts leaves one wondering how much these aids would benefit the reader of a normal, more cohesive text. We would seem to be better off to put our effort into writing more comprehensible, cohesive, and logical texts using familiar content than into teaching strategies or providing other contexts.

A few other brief comments are in order. First, it should be mentioned that Baker and Stein's discussion of story grammar fails to point out that the grammars are analytic, taxonomic descriptions of story content and are not models or theories about how a child comprehends and recalls a text. Moreover, the grammars and the research they inspire do not have explicit rationales for some of their major findings on disorganization on recall or differences in recall for different categories of story content. The fact that disorganizing a story by moving about its content leads to poor comprehension and recall could result because the disordered story separates logically and causally related events rather than preventing the use of a script or story schema. Second, the fact that settings, goals, actions, and consequences are better recalled than internal responses or reactions could result from differences in content rather than from functional differences. In a recent study by Nezworski, Stein, and Trabasso (1978), it was found that children five to eight years of age inferred motives and recalled information from settings, initiating events, internal responses, consequences, and reactions equally well when the categories were equated for content, casting doubt on the supposed importance of categories.

Inferences receive brief comment in only one review (Baker & Stein). This is a shortcoming of the field. Inferential comprehension has not been a topic of research, partly because we lack theory and analysis on what inferences are. Tentative suggestions are contained in Clark (1975); Nicholas and Trabasso (in press); and Warren, Nicholas, and Trabasso (1978) who provide taxonomies. Omanson, Warren, and Trabasso (in press) have conducted a study of memory and inferences on five and eight year old children, finding successful performance by both ages over a wide range of inferential types, including those which fill in slots between events. The basis for making inferences appears to be experimental or world knowledge rather than formal reasoning.

Finally, the reviews omit one major question: How do we learn from what we read in a text? How do we acquire new structures? The reliance upon scripts, schemata, story grammars, and prior knowledge as explanations or theories of how comprehension occurs begs this question. The work on metamemory or strategic behavior hints that learning is important but metamemory studies are not based on any learning theory. It merely says that knowledge about skills helps in choosing to use them and omits explanations about what these skills are and how they are acquired. We desperately need to know how we learn from what we read and what conditions promote this learning.

In the final section of this paper I wish to fill in a missing element of the Johnson and Barrett review, namely, what do the schools actually do in teaching or promoting comprehension skills?

As an example of practice, I would like to draw your

attention to a curriculum for teaching comprehension developed by the Montgomery County Public Schools (1974) in Rockville, Maryland.

A comparison between the methods cited in the reviews and those in the curriculum developed by the Montgomery County Public Schools leaves one with the impression that the practitioners or educational technologists are far ahead and more imaginative in procedures, goals, and methods than are basic researchers, the teacher of teachers, or the publishers of programs. The implication is obvious, namely, that persons doing research on reading comprehension should go back to the classroom and reexamine those situations in which reading and reading comprehension occur. This return to the real world would influence several aspects of research: what tasks and texts are chosen for reading as well as how understanding of these tasks or texts is to be measured.

The Montgomery County Public Schools organized their curriculum on teaching comprehension around nine goals. The goals constitute an operational definition of the products of comprehension and their realization involves content, method, and assessment, assumed to be appropriate to grades K through 12. The categories of comprehension and goals are:

1. *Word meanings.* The goal is to have the child understand what he reads by knowing what individual words mean. The basic approach is associationistic, naming of words in association with objects and ideas. The curriculum involves correct use and identification of word meanings; production of synonyms and antonyms; use of specialized words from subject matter fields; distinguishing connotative and denotative meanings; and the learning of roots of words, classes, or discriminating features as well as formal definitions. This section builds basic conceptualizations necessary to comprehending larger units of discourse. It is curious that research on vocabulary knowledge (which must increase with age and specific subject matter experiences) and reading comprehension was omitted from the reviews. Either such work is nonexistent or not in vogue. It shouldn't be hard to demonstrate a correlation between vocabulary and recall, independent of age.

2. *Location and recall.* The twin goals are the location (external) and recall (internal) of specific information. The approach recognizes that much of what is known is external to us and stresses the active seeking of information from multiple sources—newspapers, books, films, filmstrips, tapes or records, dictionaries, etc. The child is encouraged to learn to use appropriate sources. This learning involves learning their structure—the parts of a book or the organization of a dictionary or the content headings of an encyclopedia. Other text materials involve glossaries, thesauruses, telephone directories, TV guides, atlases, almanacs, magazines, pamphlets, brochures, catalogues, advertisements, and concert or theater programs. This listing should make us aware of the range of communication materials which require reading comprehension. Since the structure and task demands of these vary, we may wonder whether the comprehension processes are general or specific. My guess is both, and that different media or forms of communication require special knowledge for understanding.

As far as recall is concerned, the children are encouraged to write or remember the content they seek in these sources. This involves notetaking, constructing and use of representation of information although what scripts appear here seem quite varied. We note also that very little verbatim recall is required since the material read clearly exceeds limitations of surface retention. The current stress on free (verbatim) recall or at least recall of surface content finds little place in this curriculum.

3. *Translation.* The goals here are for the child to be able to transcribe or translate between different forms or representations of communication. Activities involve translation from pictures or words and vice versa or following directions from pictures or words, acting out through body language, theatrical instructions, recoding dialects, reducing figurative or literal description via interpretation of fables, proverbs, morals, etc. and paraphrasing or illustrating or summarizing materials from one level of abstraction to another.

This category contains what Johnson and Barrett as well as Levin and Pressley refer to as paraphrase but the contrast in richness is striking. The representation of information in different modes, following directions, acting out, translating into own words, giving examples and summarizing all seem, intuitively, to be good procedures to measure comprehension. One question of interest is whether or not they are measures of a common representation or set of abilities. Could researchers use more than one of these measures for a common text or communication and look for individual differences? Are some translation abilities dependent upon development? Does translation help subsequent comprehension?

4. *Interpretation.* Here, the goal is to get children to relate ideas. One approach stresses identification of main ideas, themes, or issues, the outlining of ideas which are relevant to the theme, the identification of facts, truths, possibilities, fantasies, unrealities, impossibilities, incongruities, opinions, values, value judgments, elements of a plot, premises, stated and unstated assumptions, hypotheses, evidence, arguments, and conclusions. In addition to such identification, organization of ideas is stressed by allowing the child to compare ideas for similarity, identity, differences and contradictions. Classification, analogy, inference, implication, conclusion and generalization occur as well as identification, production and recognition of cause and effect relations.

This listing indicates that we are just beginning with the work on main ideas, inferences, and causality to tap into a rich area of comprehension. The goals here seem to be more grade level dependent than others and developmental studies which test the assumed level might be useful.

5. *Prediction.* The goal here is to help the child learn to make predictions from data where the data are narratives or sequences of events. This category demonstrates understanding through what has been termed "slot-filling" inferences and what is studied in story production (Stein & Glenn, 1977). In it, outcomes, consequences, actions, and reactions of characters are predicted. My impression is that the work on story grammars and story production is focusing on this aspect of comprehension. The reviews did not cite it because much of it is forthcoming.

6. *Application.* The goal here is to develop problem-solving skills in children. That is, the goal is to teach them to

apply what they read to new situations. This involves problem analysis, generation of solutions, planning, and deciding as well as "metacognition" skills such as justifying and specifying the limits of one's ability to solve the problem.

This category strikes me as overlapping with the others but the focus on reading as problem-solving may be both practical and representative of why we read. It is more than just a problem of following directions for it gets at creativity. The study of problem-solving and reading comprehension as joint enterprises has not been done (to my knowledge) by psychologists.

7. *Analysis.* This category involves goals which are more literary in character. Analysis is of narratives, plot, character development, literary forms, genre, point of view, tone, mood, purpose, style, values, and structure. This topic received discussion by Johnson and Barrett but little is known on its utility. The work on narratives cited by Stein and Glenn is a start in this area but it seems restricted only to simple stories. What is the child's conception of a story should be one central purpose of this area. The potential is there given the initial work on story grammars. Another question for research would be to investigate the value of knowledge of literary aspects to comprehension of narratives. Does literary analysis help one's comprehension or is it a specialized knowledge domain? Does it affect production or writing?

8. *Synthesis.* The goal here is to develop creative integration of ideas through expression, communication, and problem-solving.

This portion of the curriculum stresses writing and is taught largely in grades seven through twelve. Does writing about a subject help comprehension? We understand so little about writing as a process that it is difficult to formulate researchable questions other than simplistic, functional ones such as that above. This area is probably the least understood from a research point of view and was unmentioned in the reviews. The nascent work on information integration of narrative content (Lane & Anderson, 1976; Surber, 1977) or inferences (Paris, 1975) is of interest here.

9. *Evaluation.* This category stresses the personal evaluation of communications by the child through the establishment and use of standards or criteria for evaluation (accuracy, consistency, data adequacy, clarity, relevancy, and validity), literary standards (rules for form, genre, plot structure, development or resolution, setting, character delineation, motivation or development, tone or mood, style, and literary language), and evaluation of other techniques (advertising, editorial, and political).

This category purports to teach just what I am supposed to be doing in this chapter, namely, evaluating the work of others. I doubt that I could articulate all the criteria I have used but relevancy and validity seem to have the highest weighing in my scheme. We may wonder how children acquire and use evaluative skills in reading and comprehending communication. Is this a "metacognitive" skill or is it crucial to comprehension in general? Do we readily form opinions? In studies of moral development (Kohlberg, 1969; Rest, 1975) children evaluate characters in stories and make decisions about outcomes according to some sort of internalized standards. This clearly is a form of comprehension and the application of story grammars to this area would seem fruitful (Grueneich, 1978).

There we have it—nine categories of teaching comprehension. I think that the reader will agree with me that the research on reading comprehension and teaching of reading comprehension suffers by comparison. I hope that my message has a constructive effect, namely, that researchers examine what they mean by comprehension by studying curriculum such as that adopted by the Montgomery Public Schools (1974). From this, converging operations on the concept should emerge as well as a new set of questions for the study of the development and teaching of reading comprehension skills. If the research uses reading situations that have ecological validity, it is more likely to have relevance to educational and practical, everyday life situations.

A Retrospective Reaction to Prose Comprehension

P. David Pearson
University of Illinois at Urbana-Champaign

This paper is a reaction to the three papers that were prepared for this volume, authored respectively by Baker and Stein, Levin and Pressley, and Johnson and Barrett, with special emphasis given to the Levin and Pressley article. This discussion is divided into several sections. In the first, I speak directly to Levin and Pressley's offering—often underscoring a point they have made, sometimes taking issues with one of their conclusions, and at times pointing out an omission in their treatment. The second part is a briefer replication of part 2 for the Baker and Stein and Johnson and Barrett articles. In the third section, I have tried to raise some general issues about research and practice in prose comprehension that we all need to examine if we are to improve our models, materials, and methods for teaching comprehension.

Levin and Pressley

The Framework

Grice (1975) speaks of a set of tacit contracts between

This work was completed while Professor Pearson was a Visiting Scholar Professor at the Wisconsin Research and Development Center for Individualized Schooling at the University of Wisconsin, Madison. It was supported by the National Institute of Education under contract No. US-NIE-C-400-76-0116 (Center for the Study of Reading) and under Center contract No. 08-NIE-G-78-0217 (Wisconsin Research and Development Center for Individualized Schooling).

117

author and reader. Pearson and Johnson discuss comprehension as an active dialogue between the writer and reader. Levin and Pressley make a similar distinction when they divide prose strategies into "those that authors can use to optimize communication (i.e., prose-dependent strategies); and those that learners can use to optimize reception (i.e., processor-dependent strategies)." Their second independent classification vector—*stage setting strategies* versus *storage/retrieval strategies*—while not quite as tidy as the first, has some heuristic value for classroom teachers. It should allow them to classify strategies they use with children according to when, in the conduct of a reading lesson, they ought to be emphasized.

I see one problem in such a two way classification system, at least from the point of view of what teachers often do during reading lessons. If *stage-setting strategies* occur *before* reading and *storage/retrieval strategies* occur *during* reading, where are we to place the myriad of discussion, interaction, studying, refinement, and rereading activities that teachers can and do use with some students *after* reading a selection? If one has a goal of maximizing the likelihood that a student will learn what is in a text, it seems that what teachers and students do after reading may be equally as important as what they do while students read or before students read. I would modify their scheme to include post-reading study strategies under the *storage/retrieval* rubric for *processor-dependent* strategies. Indeed, I think they must have had such a modification in mind; witness the fact that they included writing summaries (a post-reading strategy) in this category.

Nonetheless, the two way classification scheme—given the inherent problems that Levin and Pressley pointed out and the one I have added—seems useful. And they were able to classify a large number of strategies from research studies into each of their four cells.

A Teacher's Point of View

Though I am no longer a classroom teacher, my dealings with classroom teachers on a daily basis in an instructor/advisor role have given me some sensitivity toward their views of theory and research (mostly derived from implicit and explicit complaints about the essential irrelevance of my graduate methods courses). At any rate, I have tried to examine the Levin/Pressley paper from a teacher's point of view.

Indeed the teacher is not highlighted in their strategy classification scheme. The teacher does exist in the scheme implicitly. I think Levin and Pressley would argue that the teacher's roles are 1) to teach students to use *processor-dependent strategies* that work and avoid those that do not, and 2) to select materials that demonstrate good *prose-dependent strategies*. In their closing paragraph they allude to one of these roles when they suggest that ". . . potentially effective prose learning strategies require clever delivery on the part of an instructor . . ." (p. 31). But such advice falls short of providing the kind of experimentally and clinically validated directions for intervention that many if not most teachers might like.

In fact, Levin and Pressley—and, for that matter, Baker and Stein and Johnson and Barrett—are noticeably cautious in the direct advice they give to teachers. All tend to use qualifiers like "possible," "potential." and "tentative." There is good reason for their caution. For while there do exist many possible implications for practice from one research study to another, the implications suffer in three dimensions.

First, as Levin and Pressley point out, the conclusions (and hence the implications) differ from one study to another.

Second, many of the implications can and should be validated experimentally in classroom situations before we make any plans for widescale adoption. For example, Levin and Pressley report considerable evidence to support the conclusion that what a reader brings to a passage greatly influences what he or she takes away from it in the form of recall or comprehension (Davidson, 1976; Brown, Smiley, Day, Townsend, & Lawton, 1977; Gordon, Hansen, & Pearson, 1978). A possible implication of this research is that specific schema-building instruction (in the form of vocabulary, concept, or semantic network activities) prior to reading should enhance comprehension of a passage.

Such a suggestion is hardly surprising to us; it fits our intuitive feelings about the value of such instruction. Yet it is one thing to demonstrate that *existing* schemata, developed naturally over time and/or invoked for a particular selection, facilitate comprehension; it is quite another to demonstrate that specific teacher directed activities designed to alter readers' schemata for a particular topic will have a similar effect.

Third, many of the implications suggested in the Levin and Pressley and Baker and Stein papers are only incidentally important for teachers; they are really directed at publishers and curriculum developers since they deal more with materials than instructional strategies. Teachers can avail themselves of these implications only in their materials selection function *and* only if the publishing industry responds to the conclusions drawn in papers like those in the present volume.

Lest I dwell excessively on the "cautious" side of Levin and Pressley's offering, let me offer my conviction that there is much to be gleaned by a classroom teacher from their review.

Levin and Pressley close their review by pointing out the inconsistencies from one study to the next. One study's "champ" is a second's "chump," they say. These inconsistencies stem largely from the fact that different "situational constraints" are controlled or uncontrolled from one experiment to the next. In such a state of affairs it is tempting to conclude that our research is inconclusive due to our lack of scientific rigor. But this same state of affairs probably seems reasonable to a teacher who is used to making instructional decisions in a highly interactive environment—in an environment where the success of an instructional strategy depends upon factors like the difficulty and structure of the content, the demands of the task, and a host of individual student characteristics. In other words, if teachers regard the Levin and Pressley paper as a catalog of promising and partially successful ideas that need to be validated in their own classroom ecologies, then they will definitely benefit from the ideas presented. What is missing, what teachers will have to add, are the specific details of the general strategies described in the Levin and Pressley paper.

Perhaps all this is but another way of saying that our

prose comprehension research is still in a relatively primitive stage. Indeed one of the distinguishing characteristics of an established versus a novitiate science is the level of specificity that the established science can provide to explain and predict phenomena. To those who would argue that research like that reviewed by Levin and Pressley adds nothing new to a teacher's repertoire of instructional strategies—that they have succeeded in verifying the obvious—I would counter in two ways. First, I tend to be quite suspicious of research which concludes by recommending prose-learning strategies that are counter-intuitive. There is no good reason to expect research to reveal surprises; indeed, it ought to corroborate our best intuitions and reasoning. Second, as I have already argued, as our research becomes more sophisticated, our conclusions and recommendations will become more specific. For example, now we can say that stage-setting strategies help, sometimes more so, sometimes less so, depending upon several factors. A decade from now we may be able to specify particular conditions. In other words, the main ideas we now offer to teachers may not differ from their own intuitions. And they may not change in the future, but the "details" we generate in the future may be quite novel.

Some Specific Issues

Stage-setting strategies. One of Levin and Pressley's points regarding content-clarifying strategies (a subclass of *processor-dependent stage-setting strategies*) deserves special emphasis and expansion. They point out that such strategies seem to help when the material to be read is "difficult to comprehend (abstract, unfamiliar, or ambiguous) . . ." for a particular student. For the past two or three years at Minnesota, we have been trying to specify the boundary conditions for such pre-reading instructional activities. Like so much of the research reported by Levin and Pressley, we get different findings from one study to the next. For example, Swaby (1977) found that an intensive vocabulary development (really concept development) treatment was superior to an advance organizer or read-only control treatment, but only for *below average readers* reading reasonably *familiar* material. Schachter (1978), on the other hand, found that a somewhat similar treatment was uniquely effective for *above average readers* reading relatively *unfamiliar* material.

These inconsistent findings lead me to conjecture that it is not difficulty *per se* that renders a passage appropriate for content-clarifying strategies. Instead it is an optimal level of difficulty. If a passage is too simple (as it might have been for the above average students in Swaby's study), then such strategies are superfluous.

If the content of the passage is too difficult or novel (as it might have been for the below average readers in Schachter's study), such vocabulary instruction may not "take." There simply may be too little in the way of preexisting semantic network to build on.

Verbatim/paraphrase distinction. I want to take issue with the emphasis that Levin and Pressley have given to the verbatim/paraphrase question distinction. First, after Anderson (1972), they argue that paraphrase (different words or syntax than in the text) questions measure comprehension, whereas verbatim (same words and syntax as in the text) measure something like simple rote recall. They go on to point out that adjunct pictures facilitate both verbatim and paraphrase question-answering behavior, whereas simple story repetition facilitates only verbatim question answering.

To suggest that verbatim questions measure rote recall surprises me. Surely, if such a conclusion is drawn, it can only be drawn for very, very short text segments. Otherwise we would have to assume that readers hold the surface structure of text verbatim in working memory. The conclusion might also be drawn where students are allowed to look back at a text while answering a question. But what is measured in such circumstances is not so much rote recall as it is student ability to engage in orthographic and syntactic search strategies. In fact if one believes (as most people seem to these days) that the surface structure of a text is interpreted (or possibly converted to semantic primitives) as information travels from short term to long term memory, then one is forced to speculate that both paraphrase and verbatim questions will have to undergo some sort of recoding transformation when a subject tries to compare it to information stored in long term memory. If this is true, then paraphrase and verbatim questions ought to differ in difficulty only insofar as paraphrase questions employ more difficult, unfamiliar or ambiguous words or phrases. If it is true, as they conclude, that adjunct pictures are comparatively more helpful for paraphrase than verbatim questions (when compared to the absence of pictures), it is likely to be because pictures help with more difficult probes rather than because pictures are more helpful when a "better" measure of comprehension is used.

I have another concern about that same conclusion. They conclude that pictures are useful for both types of question probes while passage repetition is useful only for verbatim questions. But the data they have marshalled better supports the conclusion that pictures are more helpful in general. In other words, their conclusion implies an interaction between level of aid and question type. But such an interaction is present in only one (Ruch & Levin, 1977) of the four studies cited in this section of the paper. In the other, pictures appear to be better than textual repetition across both question types.

A Final Word about the Levin and Pressley Paper

I am favorably impressed with the Levin and Pressley contribution. Many of the reasons for this impression should be obvious from my review. But the section I like best is their concluding section. It possesses the appropriate balance of caution about drawing instructional implications too soon, criticism of our research shortcomings, and optimism about our future in both research and instruction in prose comprehension.

Baker and Stein and Johnson and Barrett

Baker and Stein

The Baker and Stein offering differs from the Levin and Pressley paper in several ways. Most notable is its direct emphasis on developmental patterns of growth in prose comprehension skills (as opposed to the emphasis on direct efforts to improve prose comprehension inherent in the Levin and Pressley article).

A second difference involves the way the two groups of authors have chosen to divide up the world of prose comprehension into skills and strategies. This difference underscores a classic difficulty in communication about comprehension, one that Johnson and Barrett emphasize early on in their article.

I find little to disagree with in the Baker and Stein paper. They have marshalled an impressive array of evidence to support their conclusions. And they have exercised appropriate caution in jumping toward unwarranted implications for classroom instruction. But I do want to amplify two issues that they have raised: 1) The whole issue of what a main idea is and 2) the relationship between prior knowledge and the logical structure of text.

Main ideas have always puzzled me. I concur in the judgement of Baker and Stein that the research completed upon main ideas is confusing because people use the term to refer to somewhat different entities. The research seems almost as confusing as instructional practices in the field. The basic problem is that the term "main idea" is but a main idea for a polyglot of tasks and relations among ideas. For example, in several of the studies reported by Baker and Stein, an idea was a main idea to the extent that it was related to the theme of the selection (Korman, 1945, cited in Yendovitskayz, 1971). In other studies, main ideas were those judged to be most important (e.g., Brown & Smiley, 1977). In a few others, what was meant by main ideas were the "most general" ideas in the text (e.g., Otto, Barrett, & Koenke, 1969). Surely there will be times when one idea meets all three of these criteria; yet, there will be times when a general idea is neither important nor thematic. Conversely there will be times when the most important idea is not the most general (e.g., a crucial action in a story). Relevant to the Baker and Stein paper, these variant underlying definitions of main idea make it difficult to interpret the trends they suggest at the end of the section on main ideas; one simply cannot be sure to which facet of main idea these trends apply. Nonetheless, I am forced by their evidence to infer that, by any definition, main ideas are better remembered than details.

The section on understanding logical structure is intriguing. Its relations to the sections on inference and higher order knowledge structures is intimate. Let me elaborate. To understand the logical relations among textual ideas, students must see the causal, temporal, and attributional links between those ideas. When those links are made explicit (e.g., with cue words like *because, so, then,* or *as an example*), little inference is required. However authors frequently fail to make explicit such linkages, thereby placing an inferential burden on the reader. Understanding logical structure is also highly related to understanding higher order knowledge structures in the text (i.e. story schemata) since the basic episodes in a story are usually linked temporally if not causally. In other words, higher order structures are *logical* structures, too. Baker and Stein (p. 3) are right to point out the considerable interdependence among their four skill categories; I would have made even more of an issue out of the overlap.

One other comment about logical structure. Baker and Stein argue that ". . . if children do not understand how two events in the physical world are logically related, we can hardly expect them to perceive this relationship in a text." Such an argument is presented to point out how such understandings are firmly rooted in prior knowledge of the world. I will readily grant that research demonstrates that prior knowledge consistently facilitates comprehension and recall (Brown & Smiley, 1977; Anderson et al., 1977; Gordon, Hansen, & Pearson, 1978); yet I believe that there are situations in which readers can grasp (or even learn) a relationship for which they have limited prior knowledge. My belief stems from the assumption that children are capable of learning certain metacomprehension skills, namely those derived from Grice (1975) principles about the implicit textual contracts between author and reader.

Let me illustrate. Grice principles suggest that readers have a right to assume that writers do not act capriciously. Hence, if writers place sentences (1) and (2) or (3) and (4) in adjacent slots in a paragraph, they license readers to assume an explanatory relationship between the two.

(1) John fell on the ice and broke his ankle.

(2) Susan had tripped him with her skate.

(3) Henry's car wouldn't start.

(4) James had pulled out three spark plug wires.

Furthermore writers have the option of cuing the explanatory relationship by interposing a causal link like *because* or *since* between the propositions and/or placing them in the same sentence. I conjecture that writers are particularly disposed to exercise this option when they suspect their readers might not have the experience appropriate for drawing the causal inference — e.g., in (3) and (4) as opposed to (1) and (2).

Surely all mature readers have encountered textual explanations for which they have limited, if not inadequate, prior knowledge. Surely, too, mature readers occasionally learn something new about the world from such encounters with text (put yourself in the place of reading a magazine article about a new breakthrough in medical treatment of a disease). Immature readers must encounter similar circumstances, for example, in reading history or science texts. I will grant that understanding will be better as a function of better developed schemata, but I am unwilling to grant that no understanding or new learning is possible without well-developed schema, even for young children. In fact, a recent study by Neilsen (1977) demonstrates that fifth grade students are equally capable of drawing causal inferences between textually adjacent propositions in concrete familiar and abstract-unfamiliar passages. And Gordon, Hansen, and Pearson (1978) have demonstrated that recognition of causal linkages is possible for average second grade readers without direct cuing (e.g., terms like *because, since, so*), but that it is enhanced quite dramatically when relations are made explicit by including cues, especially for students with limited prior knowledge about the topic. These two studies indicate that children are capable of applying Grice principles to text, but that they receive even more aid by direct cuing. In short, these results support Baker and Stein's claim (prior knowledge does help), but go on to suggest that students can cope with text when prior knowledge is weak if authors exercise options available to them to make explicit certain relationships, like causality.

A final word about the Baker and Stein paper. Like certain aspects of the Levin and Pressley offering, it has many implications that are more appropriate for those who write children's materials than for teachers. These represent the recommendations that I find most useful and most likely to have a rather immediate impact if taken seriously by educational publishers.

Johnson and Barrett

The Johnson and Barrett paper is a major departure from the others. It is not a review of existing research; it is itself a piece of descriptive research about the prevailing conventional wisdom in teaching so-called comprehension skills and tasks.

Since it is the book that I coauthored with Johnson that is used, along with other sources, to create the "criterion" taxonomy against which basal reader and reading methods text suggestions are compared for completeness, I find myself in the ignoble position of having to critique my own thinking regarding a scope of tasks (or activities or skills, as you will) appropriate for defining reading comprehension instruction.

What Johnson and I tried to do in the recent comprehension book (Pearson & Johnson, 1978) was to define tasks and activities given to children as much as possible in terms of textual variables. In fact, we began the book by criticizing other taxonomies for indiscriminately interweaving textual and cognitive variables in their lists, thus leading to a classic "apples and oranges" problem. We succeeded in this attempt to a limited degree. The first nine tasks in Johnson and Barrett's list of criterion tasks reflect a textually-based set of relationships that can and do obtain between propositions. The other two derived from the Pearson and Johnson text, fact and opinion and bias in writing style, are murkier; that is, it is not clear whether these variables operate in text or in a reader's mind. I must admit that the same criticism that applies to other taxonomies also applies to ours. Johnson and Barrett muddy the water even more when they add such tasks as author's craft, mental images, literary form, and punctuation—tasks in which the underlying phenomena are sometimes in a writer's mind. However, in making such a criticism of their criterion tasks, I must accept some of the responsibility.

Comments about their criterion list aside, let me turn to their methodology. They offer two important limitations about their methodology, to which they should have added a third. They admit that by sampling from only grade three and grade five texts, they may have missed some skills that were emphasized earlier or later in the series. Second (as they admit), they used only an inclusion/exclusion criterion rather than an emphasis criterion for determining what was taught. Such a technique is likely to lead to a misleading picture of comprehension instruction, especially when comparing two grades. Third, by emphasizing task inclusion and exclusion, they limited themselves to an analysis of student independent practice (i.e., they really are determining whether or not students complete worksheets or workbook pages on these tasks) and side stepped the issue of what teachers actually teach, if anything. It would have been instructive to compare *practice* emphasis versus *instructional* emphasis (what the manuals suggest to teachers by way of interaction or direct teaching strategies). This third methodological criticism leads to a broader issue of what we mean by comprehension instruction and whether any occurs at all (see Durkin, 1978, for example, for a devastating description of the *lack* of any real comprehension instruction in elementary classrooms).

What about their conclusions? Not surprisingly, they found when they examined basal readers that some tasks, like main ideas, sequence, and causality get taught a lot and others, like mental imagery and anaphoric relations, are almost never taught. The conclusions from their analysis of reading methods text are remarkably similar. One is tempted (fortunately, Johnson and Barrett are not) to chastise instructional programs for their imbalance. But caution is called for. It may be that the initial selection of criterion tasks was inappropriate. It may be that tasks such as anaphoric relations and mental images, while an important part of any construct of reading comprehension, do not require any direct instruction; this is, they may be aspects of comprehension that develop quite naturally in the broader growth of linguistic and cognitive competence. To teach them explicitly might create more confusion than order. I doubt that this is true. Indeed, I suspect that direct instruction in tasks like anaphoric relations might prove beneficial; but we simply do not have the data base, either from this paper or others, to answer the question.

I was pleased to see Johnson and Barrett separate the issue of instructional strategies from comprehension tasks. Yet clearly they did not conduct anything like a descriptive survey of instructional strategies. For reasons cited earlier, I regard this failure as unfortunate. It is interesting to me that Johnson and Barrett conclude that teacher questions form the backbone of instructional strategies for prose comprehension; Durkin (1978) excluded questioning from direct instruction, choosing to label it as assessment (a possibility that Johnson and Barrett suggest but fail to endorse). My own view on this issue (i.e., whether questioning counts as instruction) is that indiscriminate questioning of petty textual details provides a low level of assessment. On the other hand, a carefully considered set of questions—a set that *leads* students from one point of knowledge to another—can be an excellent instructional strategy and can help students to learn to read critically (for examples of what I have in mind, see chapters 8 and 9 of Pearson and Johnson, 1978, and Collins, 1977).

Some General Thoughts and Themes

I find it difficult to develop many themes or other kinds of syntheses from the three papers. Perhaps, this is as it should be; perhaps, this difficulty reflects the fact that each paper addresses a different aspect of (or set of issues related to) prose comprehension. I doubt it. Comprehension is too pervasive a phenomenon to allow for such a lack of redundancy. Rather, I suspect that differences in world view, methodology, and terminology across the three papers provide a better explanation of the difficulty I had extracting common themes. Nonetheless, a few arise.

Background Knowledge

All three papers emphasize the importance of background knowledge about the world, about the structure of text, and/or about the task as important determinants of comprehension. Of these three kinds of background knowledge, Levin and Pressley and Johnson and Barrett are inclined to regard general world knowledge as most important. Baker and Stein also see world knowledge as important, but only they emphasize the importance of knowledge about text structure. Trabasso, in his review (this volume), emphasizes the importance of world knowledge over knowledge about text structure. I am inclined to agree with all those authors. In fact, I am convinced that one of the important experiments that needs doing is to determine whether simply increasing children's funds of conceptual knowledge is more effective than any amount of specific skill practice in facilitating prose comprehension. It may be that the best way to help children comprehend better is to help them understand their world better.

Methodological Concerns

I include this section because I fear that some readers may be inclined to minimize the applicability of results obtained from studies that use what seem to be specially tailored or "rigged" materials: Materials, for example, wherein important statements are moved around in the text at what seems to be the experimentor's whim. Materials that are purposely written to be ambiguous. One can claim that such manipulations render the studies ecologically invalid in trying to draw implications for the classroom. People don't write that way, at least not for children (or except for psychological experiments).

I agree with this criticism to a certain extent. I do not want to see educators make wholesale changes in materials and instructional strategies until and unless the results of basic research have been corroborated in real classrooms, with the usual run-of-the-mill materials available, and with typical students.

But to argue that experimenters should never use materials that have been especially prepared for an experiment would be to deny the precision and control that scientists need in order to determine what aspects of texts make a difference in comprehension. One cannot conclude that adherence to canonical story structure aids story comprehension unless one has determined that violations in that structure interfere with comprehension. One cannot illustrate the power of a reader's preexisting schemata in text interpretation without providing text that invites at least two interpretations (i.e., is ambiguous).

Also, such criticisms of "rigged" materials assume that there is something natural or special or sacrosanct about text that is available in books, stories, or texts. It is at least possible that some writers have been following ill-conceived guidelines in writing for children. Rigged text may be no worse than some that already exists, and it may lead to findings that allow the publishing industry to prepare better materials.

A Message to Publishers

Another common theme is that there is enough knowledge available about the structure of text and comprehension tasks to allow publishers to modify the materials they produce for children to read and practice. Such messages are most explicit in the Baker and Stein paper, rather directly implied by Levin and Pressley, and indirectly implied in the Johnson and Barrett offering. Publishers need to consider manipulations such as the following: 1) Using only well structured stories early in instruction. 2) Highlighting main ideas and important information in stories and paragraphs by placing the information in a conspicuous location and directing readers' attention to it. 3) Clarifying logical relations between text segments through careful sequencing of propositions and manipulating explicit cuing of such relations. 4) Altering the balance of tasks practiced by children in the independent practice components of basal and supplementary materials.

A Guarded Message to Teachers

As a final comment, let me address an issue discussed earlier. All the authors have made a few suggestions about how classroom teachers might utilize the implications derived from their reviews. But each set of authors has been appropriately cautious. I think such caution is necessary. Nevertheless, for a teacher willing to regard these guidelines as "ideas worth trying out," each article has something to offer a classroom teacher searching for better ways of helping children understand text.

A skeptic might look at these guidelines (e.g., the importance of establishing prior knowledge) and cry, "old wine in new bottles." Indeed there is much in the papers to invite such criticism. But let me warn against such pessimism. It is inevitable that good research should corroborate what good teachers have been doing, almost by intuition, for decades. What would shock me would be a program of research that provided us with counter-intuitive conclusions. Second, the value of good research will not be in the general directions it offers us, but rather in the specific details and boundary conditions it gives. For example, good research will confirm the intuition that prior knowledge facilitates prose comprehension, but it will go on to specify conditions and types of students for which and whom it helps a lot, a little, and not at all.

To complete the metaphor, we may get "old wine in new bottles," but the appelation controllé will be better. Before, all we knew was that the wine came from France. As our research improves, we will know that it is from the fourth vineyard of Chateaux Giscours in the Commune Labarde in the Haut-Medoc area of the Bordeaux region. Hopefully, such knowledge will allow us to become more discriminating consumers.

Research and the Reality of Reading

Marjorie Seddon Johnson
Temple University

Introduction

The history of reading comprehension as an area of study extends back at least to the early twentieth century. Thorndike (1917 a,b) is usually credited with having focused attention on the thinking or reasoning demands of the reading situation. However, one might easily get the impression, after reading the preceding chapters, that concern with comprehension was a new development. In fact, Baker and Stein stated that "it is only within the past decade that comprehension has gained wide-spread attention as a domain of study." This seems to indicate the possibility that one problem with current investigations of and instruction in comprehension is that they are proceeding without the perspective that could come from consideration of earlier works in the area. Although there is obviously much yet to be learned, there is much information available to provide a firm basis for both research and instruction.

Without reviewing all of the literature related to comprehension, one can make several points about the directions it has taken. Thorndike's initial focus was on making an analysis of the ideas readers got from their contact with text—what they understood it to mean. He looked at both expected or "correct" responses and unexpected or "wrong" responses which they gave. He then attempted to infer the reasons for those responses.

This tradition of analysis of responses as a source of information about what a reader understands and how he functioned to arrive at that understanding has continued into the present. From the work of Thorndike, through that of other early researchers such as Carroll (1926) and Richards (1929), to current miscue analysis (Goodman, 1965) the same message has recurred—one must look carefully at the readers, the text, and the interactions among them. Comprehension is not capricious; it is the result of the interaction of a variety of determinants.

Within a short period of time after Thorndike's "beginning," attention in reading research and instruction had shifted away from word recognition and oral reading to comprehension and silent reading. Many studies appeared which were designed to yield information on a variety of questions about reading comprehension. Perhaps the most important emphasis in these early studies, and one which many succeeding studies have pursued, was the attempt to determine the nature of the relationships among specific comprehension abilities.

One of the first questions examined was that of the relationship between literal or factual comprehension and critical or interpretive. The initial emphasis was on factual vs. inferential thinking in reading with investigators such as Bedell (1934), Dewey (1935), Feder (1938), and Tyler (1930) emphasizing the fact that ability to respond in terms of specifically stated ideas was no guarantee of ability to infer on the basis of those ideas. Others looked at additional aspects of "going beyond the facts" (Davis, 1941; Gans, 1940; Irion, 1925; Langsaun, 1941; Maney, 1952; Richards, 1929; Sochor, 1941). In general, all of the studies of this type tended to demonstrate that beyond the *getting* of ideas were areas of seeing relationships, evaluating ideas, making judgments, generalizing and concluding, and solving problems.

Interest immediately developed in the relationships among the various types of abilities involved in reading comprehension. Along with many subjective analyses of the component abilities (for example, Anderson & Davidson, 1925; Gray, 1919), a series of factor analytic studies was undertaken. Many of these took

Johnson

student performances on existing reading tests and attempted to determine what factors (types of abilities) emerged from the analysis (Feder, 1938; Hall & Robinson, 1945; Langsaun, 1941). Davis (1941, 1944) and Gans (1940) used tests specifically designed to measure abilities which they viewed as important ones in reading. Conclusions about the comparative independence of various comprehension abilities were somewhat equivocal and Davis (1968, 1972) continued to explore these relationships. In general, the picture which has emerged seems to indicate much of the variance in comprehension is accounted for by a minimal number of "basic" abilities which pervade all understanding of text. However, specific abilities involved in going beyond the facts appear to be relatively independent.

Another angle which was pursued was that of whether comprehension abilities were general (that is, applicable to materials regardless of literary type and subject matter) or specific to particular fields. Artley (1942), Bond (1938), Irion (1925), Shores (1940), and Swenson (1942) all found that although there were many abilities in common across literary types and subject matter fields, there was also enough variation in comprehension across fields and types to suggest that there was some differentiation of abilities.

A more recent question is whether or not comprehension abilities are hierarchical in nature. Much of the interest in this area seems to have been sparked by the various taxonomies or classification systems of comprehension abilities and/or questions (Barrett, 1976; Bloom, 1956; Hittleman, 1978; Otto, Chester, McNeil, & Meyers, 1974; Pearson & Johnson, 1978; Ruddell, 1974; Sanders, 1966). Confusion exists in terms of whether or not the sequences in development of comprehension abilities depend on prerequisite relationships. Certain abilities seem to arise later but not directly because earlier developing abilities are prerequisite to them.

As one views this research on various aspects of the relationships among comprehension abilities, it becomes clear that correlational techniques, including factor analysis as an extension, have been the almost exclusive tool of the researcher. The assumption here appears to have been that evidence of similar performance levels in situations requiring "different" comprehension abilities indicated that the abilities were actually the same. A high correlation between performance in understanding the author's point of view and performance in understanding a cause-effect relationship or sequence, however, does not mean that these two comprehension tasks are the same. It merely indicates the often observed phenomenon that he who does well in one area most frequently also does well in others. A basic fault, then, is that high correlation has been misinterpreted as identity.

Certain problems characterize much of this early work on reading comprehension and continue to plague today's investigators. Perhaps most important is the fact that, although in 1917 Thorndike attempted to make some analysis of *why* readers understood *what* they did, virtually all the studies have looked at the *what* of reading comprehension (the things the reader understood or did not understand). Little interest has been shown in the *how* of the reader functioning (the process used). Further, little systematic attention has been given, as comprehension has been examined, to factors such as the language of the text or the specific thinking demands made on the reader.

Many developmental studies of language comprehension, concept formation and thinking processes have proceeded concurrently with the study of reading comprehension. Much of the work on the comprehension of language was done at the word level, as in the investigations of the understanding of *more* and *less* (Donaldson & Balfour, 1968) or *before* and *after* (Clark, 1971), but also extended into such areas as the handling of anaphoric expressions (Bormuth, 1970) or conditional relationships (Strickland, 1962; Paris, 1972). Work on development of thinking processes and concepts has proceeded concurrently with Piaget taking the lead in making clinical observations of children as they pass through various stages in handling the world of things and ideas. Concept formation, and in particular, styles of categorization have received particular attention through the investigations of Bruner (1956), Goldstein and Scheerer (1941), and Sigal (1964). Much of this latter work has not been tied directly to reading comprehension and has concentrated on when or if certain thinking processes appear in normals, various deviate groups, or differing personality types.

Other investigators have concentrated on the development of certain groups of concepts, rather than on the process of concept formation or attainment. Their concern has been with what concepts develop at various levels of maturity. Causal relationships, for example, were investigated by Deutsche (1937) and Piaget (1929) among others. Perhaps the most general lesson to be learned from these studies of specific concepts is that the logic of the adult is an inappropriate yardstick to apply to the evaluation of concepts derived from a child's experience.

Considering this historical background of concern with comprehension, one would hope current efforts had extended and integrated information previously gained and provided a strong foundation for educational practice. Instead the current state seems to be characterized by the presence of many problems. Perhaps most serious among them are the following:

1. Seeming to lose sight of the fact that the basic reason for investigating comprehension and improving instructional strategies is so that learners can become self-motivating and self-directing in understanding the reading materials they contact.
2. Continuing the present confused structures of comprehension as well as inadequate definition and analysis of the tasks it entails.
3. Tending to deal with isolated or artifical elements rather than the reality of reading.
4. Stating a concern for process, but investigating and teaching for product.
5. Assuming that listening and reading comprehension can be thought of as identical.
6. Assuming that interpretation and verbal production are interchangeable.

To study comprehension and how it occurs can be fascinating in and of itself. Who has not wished to crawl inside a child and find out how he comes to understand things? The satisfaction of this intellectual curiosity, however, could never be the end of concern with comprehension. If one cares enough about comprehension to be this curious about it, one must also be concerned with helping others to be self-motivating and self-directing in the search for understanding of the varied situations they face and, specifically, the reading materials they contact.

From the standpoint of instructional strategies, this idea seems to demand a somewhat different stress from the one Johnson and Barrett (this volume) found in the references they reviewed. They found that there has been and continues to be a "standard strategy for teaching the comprehension of prose passages" which "would appear to have merit if teachers use it selectively, judicially, and creatively with the intent to help students transfer some of its elements to their personal reading strategies." It is interesting to note, however, that their summary of the steps usually involved in this strategy shows activity going forward in virtually every case on the basis of an imperative to the teacher. For example, the teacher is expected to "relate the content of the passage to the reader's background." Later in the discussion Johnson and Barrett speak of "the importance of helping readers relate the content of the passage to be read to their own storehouses of language, knowledge and experiences—their scripts or schemata." Their shift of focus is more than an accident of expression. It is illustrative of the fact that instructional strategies are often not process-learning strategies for the learner. Whether the teacher helps the children to relate the content of a particular situation to their own backgrounds is relatively unimportant. The real goals are to have them recognize the need for such a process of relating (self-motivation) and to have *them* know ways in which they can search their own backgrounds for necessary materials to relate (self-direction).

Purposes for reading is another area which Johnson and Barrett identified as a universal element in the strategies for teaching comprehension. It seems obvious that one reason for Stauffer's emphasis (1975) on the *directed-reading-thinking-activity* on the student's role in purpose setting parallels the situation of relating background and current concerns. Certainly, having readers set purposes assures more involvement in the comprehending of the present reading material. More important, however, it leads readers to independence in initiating their own reading to satisfy purposes (self-motivation) and helps them to become conscious of ways they can read to accomplish various purposes (self-direction). Stauffer speaks in terms of predicting, but the setting of purposes which the learners should be helped to do must not be confined to predicting. They must learn to size up materials in terms of what might be accomplished by reading them; set for themselves purposes which are appropriate for the particular material; decide on the reading strategies they can use to accomplish those purposes; and, finally, know when they have accomplished what they set out to accomplish.

Certainly, many other examples could be pulled from both research paradigms and instructional strategies to show the lack of attention to the goals of self-motivation and self-direction. The efforts of both researchers and practitioners must be turned to this area.

Understanding Comprehension

A clearer view of comprehension itself and how it comes about seems essential to more productive research into comprehension and to higher comprehension achievement. Although much progress has been made from the point at which the clearest available definition of reading comprehension was simply "understanding what one reads," there is still much confusion evident in attempts to analyze and define comprehension. Smith (1975), for example, differentiates *knowledge,* which "consists of *facts,* of maps and statements and labels and relations," and *skill,* which "might be regarded as the way in which knowledge is put to use, the ability to apply what we know or believe" (p. 217). Not all analyses of comprehension make this type of distinction.

Another source of confusion appears to be the lack of differentiation of certain aspects of comprehension such as the end product (understanding the main idea or realizing the effect of a certain occurrence) and the way the end product must be reached (by recognition of a stated idea in the text or by inferring the idea). Johnson and Barrett (this volume) do not list inferences as one of their 17 criterion comprehension tasks because they recognize the fact that the tasks they do list can all be dealt with at either the literal or the inferential level, "depending upon what information is explicitly or implicitly stated in the passage and what is derived from the reader's experience (script)." Most other lists of comprehension tasks or abilities do include inference as a separate area. Johnson and Barrett do, however, include the handling of anaphoric expressions as a criterion task although it seems logical that the same defense presented for the non-inclusion of inference is also applicable to anaphora. As inference can be involved in the following sequence, understanding a cause-effect relationship, or getting a main idea, so can anaphoric expressions.

Whether a particular item appears on anyone's list of critical tasks in comprehension does not appear to be the crucial matter. What seems more important is that all of the elements of comprehension be considered and that they be considered in a logical structure. One possible organization for such a consideration of comprehension is the following:

1. What are the motivating factors for comprehension? What are the issues one is trying to resolve which lead one to comprehend?
2. What are the thinking processes or cognitive activities which must be used to comprehend this material?
3. What things about the language, its structure and use, must the reader appreciate in order to comprehend this material?
4. What are the ways in which the ability to marshal and direct one's energies, to use appropriate thinking processes, and to appreciate the significance of the language can be shown?

The fact that these four points deal with different aspects of the total job of comprehension is not meant to imply that they are not closely interrelated. Quite the contrary! Each must be considered as interacting with all the others.

Motivating-to-comprehend factors. If, as Smith asserts, "comprehension exists ... when there is no residual uncertainty" (p. 34), then the things which motivate one to comprehend must be the uncertainties existing in the mind of the reader. These uncertainties rarely exist in the form of lists of "comprehension abilities" as they are ordinarily spelled out in professional texts or teachers' manuals or the various compilations of "comprehension tasks" cited by Johnson and Barrett. More often they exist in terms of the ideas included in the material and the use to which readers want to put those ideas. They are, in short, characteristically the purposes they want to accomplish through comprehending the material. For example, readers may want to know how to attract bluebirds to their property. The teacher may look at this in terms of ability to get specific details or ability to follow sequence. Independent readers must also translate their motivating uncertainty into a plan of operation for comprehending. At this point, the thinking processes and the language factors come into play. The issue becomes *how* readers must function to resolve their uncertainties to achieve their purposes. Some other types of common "motivating uncertainties" are "What's the most important thing I have to know about this?" "How does this person feel about . . .?" "Is the person serious or kidding?" "How can I build a terrarium?"

Thinking processes involved in comprehension tasks. When individuals have established motives for reading, they may be able to reach their goals through the application of one thinking process or they may need to use, in an integrated fashion, a number of related processes. Comprehension tasks might better be thought of as these thinking processes.

For example, there are specific thinking processes involved in the comprehension task usually labeled as "using context to get the meaning of a word or a phrase." Teachers often feel they are giving adequate guidance when they tell the reader to "read the rest of the sentence." However, the *processes* the reader must use to profit from the rest of the sentence or the surrounding context vary according to the types of context clues which are available. Suppose the reader meets a sentence like one of these: "I studied about raccoons, coatis, kinkajous, and pandas." or "I studied about Mercury, Earth, Neptune and Venus." The fact that four items have been placed in a series should come to ignite a process for using that placement for a clue to the meaning of unknown members of the series. For readers who have never heard of a coati or a kinkajou, the process should be one of asking themselves What is a raccoon? What is a panda? and How are they alike? and then applying that meaning, at least tentatively, to the unknowns. If the only similarity that can be derived from what they know about raccoons and pandas is that they are both animals, they can at least conclude that the coati and kinkajou are also animals. If the readers know they are mammals, their conclusions can be more precise.

By the same process with added dimensions readers could get clues to the meaning of *lithium* in a sentence such as, "We examined samples of mercury, iron, aluminum, and lithium." The process of identifying each member of the series and detecting the basic similarity in mercury, iron, and aluminum could lead to the conclusion that lithium is a metal. If readers also note that iron is lighter in weight than mercury, and aluminum is lighter than iron, they could also conclude that lithium is also a metal which is lighter than any of the others.

The overall thinking *process* then, in using placement in a series as a context clue to meaning, is one in which readers use five steps in bringing the text and prior knowledge to play on the problem. First, they must realize that placement in a series implies some sort of relationship. Second, they must identify each member of the series. Third, they must identify other relationships among the members. Finally, they must draw a tentative conclusion about the unknown member on the basis of the relationships discovered. The teacher's injunction to "read the rest of the sentence" is hardly adequate guidance for the student's development and use of this process.

One very important responsibility, therefore, which faces teachers and researchers is the careful task analysis of these thinking processes. To investigate or plan teaching strategies for use of context clues, for example, requires a thorough task analysis—careful definition of the thinking which is involved in the use of the particular clue or combination of clues important in the text. To do a complete task analysis of the learnings necessary to use *all* context clues to meaning would require exploring each type of clue in the fashion that placement in a series was examined above. With even this superficial view of series as a potential context clue, it was evident that a number of learning tasks faced the reader—building a series schema, recognizing the presence of a series, identifying known members by using appropriate information from one's background, perceiving essential similarities and other essential relationships, and drawing a conclusion. To investigate or plan teaching strategies for any other comprehension task requires a similar task analysis. What are the learning tasks which the child must master and the thinking processes through which he must go if he is to be able to get the main idea, follow the sequence, or accomplish any of the other comprehension tasks usually specified?

How well is each of these comprehension tasks defined, for instruction and research, in terms of the demands it makes on the reader? Consider the area of main ideas, a common focus in the comprehension field. Baker and Stein chose "identifying main ideas" as one of the "four most commonly explored skills." Johnson and Barrett included "main ideas—details" among their "17 Criterion Comprehension Tasks" and, in fact, gave it first place in the list of tasks generally mentioned in basal series and professional texts. Trabasso included "identification of main ideas, themes or issues" among those things stressed in the area of "interpretation." One need do only a quick perusal of research and suggested instructional strategies to see that "getting the main idea" can mean many different things. Baker and Stein's review of research into main idea comprehension revealed investigation, primarily, of ability to recall important information, to rate the relative importance of ideas or events, and to detect irrelevancy of ideas or events. Danner (1976) and Otto, Barrett, and Koenke (1969), at least in their instructions to children, asked for something different—a statement of the one thing told by all the sentences. Whether this overriding idea, the message of the whole paragraph, actually existed is somewhat unclear. To do a similar quick perusal of instructional strategies suggested, four teachers' editions for basal readers were randomly pulled from a shelf and the first labeled instance of a main idea situation was located in each. Four distinct tasks were posed to the child, all purporting to be main ideas. They were choosing the correct title for a paragraph, summarizing the events of a story, deciding on appropriate headings, and choosing from two alternatives the "message" of the story. There appears to be compelling evidence, in this series of examples from a wide variety of sources, that considerable confusion exists about what this commonly taught and investigated ability really is.

Unless instructional strategies and research paradigms are based on a careful analysis of the task of getting main ideas, there appears to be little hope of effective work in this area. Knowing the topic of a piece of material and the subtopics dealt with to elaborate the original topic represents one kind of comprehension task. Recognizing the key events in a story represents another, and detecting irrelevancies yet another. Understanding the message or moral or theme is probably a much higher level task and may require recognizing it when it is stated, or inferring it when it is not stated. However, this last task seems to be the one which could most accurately be called "getting the *main idea*." It is the only one of the examples given which clearly calls on the reader to decide what the author's *main* (chief) *idea (thought)* was. Each of the other tasks seems to be a subsidiary one, such as deciding what topic was being discussed. To understand how readers accomplish any one of these tasks requires discovering what thinking the readers must do. Helping them to accomplish these tasks requires guiding them through the necessary thinking with the aim of their making the thinking process their own.

Much the same picture exists in relation to the other abilities listed or discussed in the previous articles. "Logical relationships" do not form a neat, easily perceived group since the basis of the logic which relates them may vary greatly. Are the ideas or events related by the logic of cause-effect, the logic of relative importance, the logic of geography, the logic of similarities which lead to placement in the same category, or logic of contrast? The list of possibilities could be almost endlessly extended. The what (nature of the relationship) and the how (the thinking required to perceive that relationship) of the readers' comprehension of these "logical relationships" can vary as much as does the logic of the relationship. Careful task analysis is necessary for effective teaching of the process of thinking through the relations or revealing research into its growth. Furthermore, that analysis of the task must take into account the differences among such aspects of the overall task of following a normal relationship and unscrambling a disordered relationship. Current knowledge of the conflicts which can exist between order of mention and order of occurrence should help in pointing out some of the most basic developmental differences (Clark, 1971). Until children clearly understand the significance of *before* and *after*, they are apt to assume that the first mentioned activity is also the first in occurrence.

Language factors. Virtually every teacher recognizes spontaneously certain aspects of the language and its use which serve as cues in comprehension or present difficulties in understanding. For example, such words as *first, next,* and *last* are regularly taught as cues to sequence—cues that sequence matters and cues to the actual order of ideas or events. Even those who are unaware of the meaning of the term *anaphora* recognize that confusion about pronoun reference can interfere with understanding. These language factors must be dealt with as systematically as are the thinking processes. However, as much as they are involved in the overall comprehension of the material, they are not distinct to any one of the thinking processes or comprehension tasks. Anaphoric expressions, punctuation, and ambiguities (to select from Johnson and Barrett's criterion list) can be involved in main idea-detail relationship, causal relations, sequence, etc. Likewise, from their Table 1, paraphrase, comparison, and ambiguous statements (proposition level tasks proposed by Pearson and Johnson) and all of the items in Table 2 (Anaphoric Relations) seem to deal with the language and its structure and would appear to be involved in a variety of larger comprehension tasks. On the other hand, the 14 specific tasks presented by Hittleman clearly represent areas of concern with specific elements of the language and its use.

The interaction of these language factors with both word recognition and comprehension abilities, for example, has been pointed out in miscue research. Hood (1975–1976) recommended that when miscues of different children are to be compared, all should read identical selections so that the patterns of language would not produce differential effects. Systematic attention must be directed to these language factors in both research and instructional plans. It seems obvious that readers might know, in general, what thinking process they should use in order to accomplish a certain comprehension task but be unable to carry it out because certain language structures were either beyond their ability or actually are misleading.

One specific example of difficulty with language structures is in the area of use of context clues for meaning. Before readers can put a thinking process into action, they must get their cues about the kind of process needed from the language structure. If the clue is an appositive, readers will have to proceed differently from the way in which they will proceed if the clue is a series or a formal definition. If it is contained within the same sentence, readers can operate one way but may need a different approach if it is in another sentence, linked to the first by an anaphoric expression. Analysis of the language structure is essential to the success of the search for meaning.

Evidence of comprehension. Johnson and Barrett pointed out that comprehension can be "textually explicit, textually implicit, or scriptually implicit" depending upon what appears or is implied in the text or must be drawn from the reader's background. A question asked to check or to stimulate comprehension cannot, in itself, determine whether the thinking task is at the literal or inferential level. A "why?" question may require that the reader infer a reason or may be directly answerable from the text or scripts. In order, therefore, to determine the level at which the reader is comprehending, one must consider the text and the reader's prior knowledge as well as the question and response. Otherwise there is apt to be confusion about what the reader has actually comprehended from the text.

In like fashion, there can be confusion about what is really a comprehension process and what is evidence that a comprehension process has been used effectively. For instance, the *process* of following a sequence and understanding how to complete a particular task may be *evidenced* by the performance of the task. However, the resultant performance is not the process. In other words, building the bird house can be evidence of comprehension of the directions; comparing two trees or contrasting a feline and a canine can be *evidence* of successful comprehension of expository passages which, in themselves, involved no direct comparison or contrast. A reader may have comprehended the description of each of the trees, given separately, and be able, therefore, to compare them—*evidence* of comprehension. On the other hand, the reader's evidence may be the ability to represent each accurately in some pictorial manner.

Applications of the comprehension to other tasks may differ, then, from the comprehension itself. Lack of this differentiation causes problems in both research and instruction. Some of this confusion was evident in the Baker and Stein dissatisfaction with the means which have thus far been used in the assessment of comprehension. For example, one application of having understood a story might be the ability to complete the task of rating ideas in terms of their structural importance. However, that might not be the comprehension task the readers were attempting to accomplish.

Summary comments. A basic step in planning both research and instructional strategies, then, is to set up some logical structure within which the comprehension demands can be handled. The structure of motives to comprehend, thinking abilities necessary, language factors to be dealt with, and evidences of comprehension, is simply one possible framework within which to view comprehension. Whatever structure is established, it must take into account all the essential elements and treat their interrelationships logically if one is to be in a position to do realistic research or provide instruction which will lead to independence in comprehension.

The Reality of What Is to Be Comprehended

As a literate adult, one reads a wide variety of materials,

using greatly differing approaches to the reading, to accomplish a multitude of purposes. The motives for which one reads may be as diverse as finding a telephone number or making a decision on how to cast one's ballot. Both the motive and the characteristics of the material influence the way one reads. That is the reality of reading, and it is this reality which should occupy the attention of researchers and teachers. To look at what are merely bits and pieces, isolated or artificial elements, of this reality may be totally misleading. Baker and Stein (this volume) used an example from the Brown and Smiley (1977) study of the artificial nature of certain experimental materials: "Inspection of the story reveals that the theme-irrelevant ideas were not simply details; they were deliberately introduced into the story and were noticeably irrelevant. Thus, even though the kindergartners differentiated these two classes of information, there is no guarantee that they would be able to do so with 'unrigged' stories."

Fruitful research seems to demand real materials read for appropriate motives. Two steps which the researcher or the teacher must take before setting up plans are recognizing the motives for which the material would likely be read and analyzing the demands which comprehending that material places on the reader. Trabasso (this volume) said, "the major weakness of the research viewed is the lack of explicit reasoning behind the studies." Taking these two steps prior to research would go a long way toward overcoming his objection.

Recognition of appropriate motives. This step involves reading the potential material and, insofar as possible, viewing it through the eyes of the potential reader. If the material is being considered for use with a nine year old child, the questions are "Why would a nine year old child read this? What motive would he have? What would he expect to get from it?" Unless the actual reading is for realistic motives for the maturity level of the reader, one can hardly consider what he does a faithful representation of his reading ability. He may be able to read well for motives which are appropriate for him but be unable to perform adult type tasks with the same material.

Analysis of the demands on the reader. Having identified rational motives for the reading of material, the teacher or researcher must analyze the material to see what is demanded of the reader if he is to accomplish his goals. This analysis must take into account such factors as the specific vocabulary used, the background of information and conceptual development required, the thinking abilities which must be applied, and the organizational and language structure of the material. In each of these areas it is important to recognize what the reader must already have (what he must bring to the reading of the material), what is available through the reading of the material (through use of context clues to meaning, provision of vicarious experience, or guidance in the reorganization of concepts), and what aids the author has provided.

This analysis of the demands which the material makes on the reader is essential to meaningful research into comprehension. Unless the demands are clear, it is impossible to determine what the reader is doing successfully and where his comprehension is breaking down. If the research paradigm is one designed to determine the level of a reader's ability to get the main idea, the material should clearly be of such a nature that the reader will not be bogged down by inadequacies in other areas. If he fails to get the main idea, it should not be because he lacks the necessary background knowledge or because he cannot derive appropriate word or phrase meaning from the context clues provided. It should be material for which getting the main idea is a realistic reading motive and in which the reader will encounter no difficulty with other aspects of comprehension. The researcher, then, like the teacher must make his analysis of the material in light of what the potential reader will bring to the comprehending of material.

For the teacher, this appraisal of material in terms of the reader-to-be may be somewhat easier because of his knowledge of the information, skills and abilities which his students have. After he has analyzed the demands which the material makes on any reader, he can determine from his prior knowledge of his students whether or not it is realistic to expect them to meet these demands. He can identify which of these demands they will be able to meet independently, which they can meet with his instructional guidance, and which are impossible for them to meet. Decisions both about the appropriateness of the material and about the instructional strategies can then be made.

Efforts must be directed, then, toward both researching and teaching in realistic, purposeful and ability-appropriate reading comprehension situations. Such situations can be developed only out of a thorough understanding of comprehension and the elements which affect it.

Process vs. Product

Marshall and Glock (1978) began their report on their study of the interrelationships of certain features of text and recall with the statement that it "represents a new and rapidly growing line of research into the actual process of comprehension" (p. 11). In actuality, they hoped to be able to make "certain inferences about the organization of information in memory" and see "what aspects of text . . . are most important to the comprehension process." It appears to be true that only by this kind of inference has the matter of *process* been considered.

The *products* of comprehension are situation-specific. They lack wide transfer value. The *product* will be useful again only if one is confronted with the same comprehension task in relation to the same material. To put it more bluntly, the *answer* will have continuing value only if the same question continues to arise. It is the thinking *process* which one continues to use— that is, it is the process which one is able to transfer from one situation to another. Until the reader has acquired the necessary thinking processes, he is eternally dependent on outside guidance for his comprehension. He may have arrived at many correct answers but be unable to get another similar answer unless he is carefully guided through the thinking by teacher questions and other aids.

Common research techniques for examination of comprehension (recall, recognition, responding to questions) all seem to concentrate on the product with no specific inquiry into the process. In addition to the inferences about process which researchers can make, there appear to be various other possibilities for the study of process. One obvious way to examine the processes followed in comprehending printed materials is to use some type of introspection. In one way or another, the reader can be asked to reconstruct and report what he did to comprehend the material.

Baker and Stein (this volume) discussed current research into metacognition, understanding of the cognitive processes being used. Basic to research into processes used and instruction designed to help readers develop real self-guidance in the use of thinking processes, is prior logical analysis of those processes. Asking for introspection, particularly from very young children, may be fruitless unless some guides for that introspection, in the form of questions, are provided. One may have to ask rather specifically about particular steps of the process in order to elicit from the reader information about what he did as he manipulated the ideas and the language of the material he was reading.

Another possibility for either research-oriented or instructionally-oriented evaluation of processes used is to set up the total task so that process steps are clearly defined and structured. One step in a sequential thinking process can be, to some degree, separated from other steps so that success or failure in its accomplishment can be appraised. By this technique one may be able to identify, at least, the specific point of breakdown in the total thinking process.

From the instructional standpoint, one illustration cited by Baker and Stein (this volume) has particular relevance. First graders were unaware when their understanding of directions was adequate and when it was not. Only when they attempted to execute those directions did they find out that there was not sufficient direction given.

Knowledge of whether or not one has actually accomplished a particular comprehension task is certainly a basic element in metacognition. However, from an instructional standpoint, the judgment about whether or not the objective of reading has been accomplished is often left in the hands of the teacher. Yet, if one is to see that the reader really incorporates the necessary thinking process, *one* must have opportunities to decide whether *one* has comprehended satisfactorily and *one* must be given the chance to discuss *how* one went about accomplishing that comprehension task. There is strong evidence in every day experience to support the conclusion that good thinking processes are infrequently examined in this way in the classroom. It shows in the almost universal tendency for students to interpret questions such as "What made you think that?" or "How did you get that answer?" as signals that the answer (the product) was wrong. One can often get responders to change their answers by asking this kind of question or even by raising an eyebrow in a quizzical manner. Frequent demonstrations and discussion of successful thinking processes must become a basic part of the classroom activities of students.

Levin and Pressley (this volume) spoke to this matter of process in relation to strategies which lead to improved comprehension. They categorized those that "seem to succeed" into those that are "prose dependent" and those that are "processor dependent." They addressed process in that those strategies which are "imposed" by the very nature of the prose and those that are "induced" by instructional direction, represent a way to evolve a process by which the prose can be comprehended. Their illustration of the "stage-setting" strategy which might be used by an effective game player offers a good case in point. If the contestant has adequate world knowledge which is well organized and self-activating, he or she can do the kind of anticipating of exemplars of the class he or she must work with (French things, in their illustration). If one had no relevant world knowledge, someone would obviously have to help in the acquisition of the necessary background before one could play the game. However, one may have a background of knowledge and have no process by which to activate it. It may be that one's conceptual map is not a map at all but simply a display of unrelated knowledge. Basic processes for concept formation or categorization may have to be taught before one's experience becomes sufficiently organized to be available. Further, one may have to be given direct help on strategies for retrieving information from this organized store. Only when one has acquired processes of activation which can be applied independently will one become a successful contestant. Until this time, instruction must involve guiding one through the process with a gradual reduction of the degree of responsibility the teacher bears as the learner becomes able to carry out some of the direction independently.

The path from complete lack of a process to mastery so that it is used spontaneously and without direct stimulation may be long and complex. Perhaps one of the greatest failings of instruction directed toward the development of these strategic processes is that the assumption is made that one or two demonstrations of the process will lead to mastery. Rarely is this the case. A further complication arises when situations used for the repeated experience with the application of a particular strategy are not actually parallel cases. For example, one experience with activating relevant information from one's conceptual structure may involve what Bruner (1956, p. 41) calls a conjunctive category. In this case, asking oneself, "What other things do I know which are *like* these?" is an appropriate strategy. Once one has determined what the essential likeness is which defines the category, one can institute a search of one's background for other exemplars, other things which display this same basic likeness. However, if the next situation provided for additional use of the strategy is one which involves not a conjunctive but a disjunctive or relational category, the search for some kind of basic likeness will not be fruitful. The situation provides not another chance to use the same strategy but the necessity for the use of a different strategy.

One of the most encouraging developments in relation to prose comprehension at this time is the improved analysis of what Levin and Pressley called the prose-dependent strategies. There seems to be a greater attempt to analyze what makes materials themselves more or less understandable. Unless this is accompanied by an equal or even greater interest in the processes readers use to deal with prose, and by instructional strategies which can help readers make these processes their own, this knowledge may not lead to much improvement in comprehension.

Listening and Reading Comprehension

The relationships between listening and reading comprehension have long been the subject of investigation. Certain basic knowledge about these relationships appears to be well established. In general, listening comprehension exceeds reading comprehension through the early years, reaches a point of equality with it as reading ability increases, and often comes to be less adequate than reading comprehension in the mature reader. Many factors may be involved, not the least of which is attention, in this final preference for reading over listening for thorough understanding. The prerequisite nature of listening comprehension and comprehension in practical, real-life situations to reading comprehension can also be accepted. Until an individual has learned to use certain thinking processes in less abstract situations, that person can hardly be expected to use them in the more abstract written-language interpretation.

These relationships, however, cannot be used as a reason to use listening and reading comprehension interchangeably in research. Although this use of the two as equivalent tasks has been apparent in certain studies of comprehension, others such as Weisberg (1978) have attempted to determine what variations and commonalities might exist between specific kinds of performance based on listening and that based on reading.

A related question which requires considerably more thought and research is that of pure recall as related to comprehension when materials continue to be available. Certainly the continued availability of material, for review or rereading for additional purposes which arise, is the source of one difference between listening comprehension and reading comprehension. Certain standardized tests such as the Iowa batteries even have separate sections to measure the comprehension of reading materials on a pure recall basis and on a material available for further perusal basis. The latter would obviously appear to be the most normal kind of reading activity outside the research or instructional-bound sphere.

Comprehension and Verbal Production

A final difficulty facing both teachers and researchers is that of establishing criteria for evidence of comprehension. Much of the research has treated verbal production as evidence of comprehension—what the subject restates is what he comprehended. There are two obvious problems with verbal production as the main or exclusive measure of comprehension. The first problem, one which has been noted by Baker and Stein, is that the verbal production is far less than what has been comprehended. For example, inferences may have been drawn which seemed so obvious to readers that they failed to report them as additional parts of their comprehension. The most frequently used technique to avoid this particular difficulty has been to present inferences to see if they are "falsely recognized" as part of the original material. However, this technique immediately introduces another commonly recognized difficulty—there is no way to tell whether the readers drew the inference as a result of their reading of the material or merely recognized it as plausible when it was suggested to them. The second obvious problem is that the verbal production may represent more than what has been truly comprehended. Particular words, phrases, or sentences may be recalled without their meanings having been apprehended at all.

The strongest positive point about verbal production as a measure of comprehension is that it represents, within the above limitations, what the comprehender got from the material. Again, it seems apparent that in most out-of-laboratory and out-of-classroom reading, readers must ultimately produce their own understandings. Rarely do readers meet a situation comparable to a multiple-choice test question. No one offers them possible answers from which to choose. In fact, the hallmark of their becoming self-directing readers is that they are able to produce their own answers but also to raise their own questions.

Consideration should certainly be given to using research paradigms which include other measures of comprehension. Production rather than simply recognition should certainly be involved. However, the types of production possible are far more varied than is evident from research studies thus far. Particularly, as more investigations are made and as Baker and Stein indicated must be done with materials other than narratives, there is an obvious need to introduce other, more suitable measures as evidence of comprehension. Following a set of directions, for instance, is a better demonstration of their real comprehension than is verbal production of the directions. One must be careful in using such evidences of comprehension, however, that something like motor skills does not interfere with one's demonstration of understanding.

Conclusion

Throughout the chapters in this volume, certain problems which tend to pervade much of the research into comprehension have been mentioned repeatedly. For example, it has certainly been recognized that confusions exist between memory and comprehension, that most investigation has been of the what and when of comprehension rather than the why and how, and that research paradigms have frequently not reflected the thought about comprehension which has gone into formulation of instructional programs.

Perhaps the two most important points to be made, if research and practice are to lead to improved comprehension of all types of prose and other verbal discourse, are these: first, a much more thorough analysis must be made of the learning tasks which face the developing comprehender; second, all attention to reading comprehension must be in the context of the reality of reading. If these things are done, the results should lead much more directly to the development of readers who are competent, self-motivated, and self-directing comprehenders.

Children's Reading Comprehension:
A Final Word

Carol Minnick Santa
Kalispell Reading Project
School District No. 5
Kalispell, Montana

In this volume, we have expressed every manner of concern about children's comprehension. We have examined basic research and abstract theoretical notions about comprehension, but we also have looked at the applied issues of teaching comprehension. All the authors have to some extent tried to reflect upon and bridge the gap between the educator and the psychologist in their concern with comprehension. The range of views expressed has indeed made the work interdisciplinary in nature.

Given the different perspectives expressed in the various chapters, a few concluding remarks might be useful. These comments have two primary goals: 1) to examine the perspective of educators and psychologists in order to understand better the similarities and differences that have appeared, and 2) to extract a synopsis of thinking across contributors about the seemingly central issues.

Let us begin by considering the underlying perspective or schema that a psychologist and educator might bring to bear on the problem of comprehending comprehension.

First, a cognitive psychologist would very likely take a multiple levels approach to comprehension. According to this view, comprehension takes place on several interacting levels.

That is, it is possible to talk about comprehension or understanding single words. At the next level, one might describe the comprehension of single sentences. From here, we move to the level of the paragraph where psychologists have directed their efforts toward understanding how one sets up consistent representations of the information conveyed in a single paragraph. Practically all of the investigations referred to in the present volume were at the paragraph level of comprehension.

Beyond the representation of specific episodes of information, there is still another level of comprehension where one relates one episode of knowledge to another. At this level, we are concerned with the integration of new knowledge with all of a person's prior knowledge structures.

Research has just begun to explore this final integrative level. Current work in schema theory has already helped us understand how we use specific aspects of our prior knowledge to set up representations of incoming information. Schema theory and story grammars provide models of how we structure material as it is coming in, and give us at least a rudimentary idea of how knowledge can be related across episodes.

Finally, it is important to note that those advocating cognitive models recognize that each level of comprehension is capable of influencing the other levels. Comprehending a sentence depends upon understanding the words within the sentence. A less obvious but equally important conclusion is that "higher levels" of comprehension influence all lower levels. That is, a person's expectations and general knowledge can easily influence one's ability to understand a sentence or even a word. Similarly, a person's understanding of a paragraph will influence comprehension of each sentence which, in turn, will affect the understanding of each word in the sentence.

To summarize, psychologists consider comprehension as a process of representing incoming information at various levels. Each level of comprehension involves understanding the information with respect to a more or less circumscribed sphere of context. One understands a word with respect to the concept represented by the word, or with respect to the word fitting within a sentence, or within a paragraph, or within a person's lifetime of experience. Finally, it is important to note that many if not most current views of cognitive psychology postulate an interactive model such that each level of comprehension exerts an influence on every other level (Glass, Holyoak, Santa, 1979).

The educational model of comprehension is also concerned with multiple levels. To understand, a child must be able to comprehend the material first in terms of words and then in terms of sentences. If the vocabulary is too difficult or if the sentence structure is too far removed from the child's own language patterns, the child will be unable to extract meaning or, in other words, form internal representations of incoming pieces of information. In this case, the child will never be able to transcend the level of sentential processing to construct a representation of an entire paragraph.

In short, educators are concerned with exactly the same levels of comprehension as are psychologists. The difference between educators and psychologists is one of emphasis. Psychologists have typically focused on "lower" levels of comprehension than have educators. Even now as psychologists turn to higher levels of comprehension, we find the text is extremely simple and questions rudimentary as compared with the types of comprehension issues routinely faced by educators. However, the "levels of concern" do indeed show promise of converging.

Despite a general consensus about the various levels of comprehension there are at least two ways in which educators differ from most cognitive psychologists: 1) emphasis on individual differences and 2) a concern with motivational factors. Educators feel that any program for teaching comprehension must focus on helping individual children to comprehend. Psychologists, on the other hand, are concerned with understanding how children comprehend. That is, a psychological theory is useful only if it allows general statements about people or groups of people. Yet, a teacher must be concerned about the discrepancies between each individual child and the hypothetical average child.

Take for example, Marjorie Johnson's description (this volume) of the teacher's role in creating independent comprehending readers. Before beginning any reading lesson, the teacher must carefully examine the material to be read. The teacher determines what the likely motives will be for children reading the material, and determines the demands the material places on the child. The teacher mentally assesses the vocabulary, structure, and content of the passage and, given this analysis, evaluates her role in helping each child overcome potential difficulties in successfully reading the material. Based upon the child's motives for reading the material, and the reader's conceptual background, the teacher determines the thinking processes needed by the child for achieving his purpose. Given all of this information, the teacher is ready to introduce the material to the child. During the actual teaching, the teacher works toward making the child as independent as possible, and as the child becomes more proficient, the teacher role changes from that of instructing to that of leading the child toward establishing purpose and motivation for reading, and toward activating relevant background knowledge. Thus, we see in the educator a clinician's regard for the individual and a deep concern with developing the process of comprehension.

The educator, teaching the process of comprehension, stands in marked contrast to the psycholgist's detailed analysis of the product of comprehension. Hopefully, awareness of this difference in emphasis will expand both educators' and psychologists' understanding of comprehension. As educators attempt to teach individual children the skills of comprehension, they should draw upon psychologists' descriptions of the comprehending child and the essence of well formed representations. As psychologists continue their efforts to develop models of comprehension, they should expand their characterizations to include descriptions of the process of comprehension.

Having briefly outlined both the psychologists' and educators' views of comprehension, let us now turn to an overview of the major issues that appear in the present volume. Whenever possible we will summarize the research base underlying each topic and then draw implications for psychological research and educational practice.

Background Knowledge

As would be a logical prediction from both a research and a teaching model of comprehension, background knowledge has a very prominent status throughout this volume. There was overwhelming agreement among all of the authors that the better and more related the background knowledge, the easier it will be to comprehend. In fact, several authors felt that background knowledge may be the most important ingredient of good comprehension (Pearson, Trabasso, this volume). Such a strong conclusion is, of course, not fully supported by experimental results, but the data do suggest a very strong relationship between background knowledge and comprehension (Baker & Stein, Levin & Pressley, this volume).

Most of the research in the area falls under the rubric of schema theory and story grammars. Schemata are one's stored concepts and experiences which guide one's interpretation of new experiences. Story grammars might also be considered as a type of schema, in that they are not content specific, but general representations of structure useful for comprehending stories.

In summarizing research in schema theory, the evidence is sufficiently compelling to conclude that the quality of one's schema is related to comprehension. A person's schema seems to determine one's success in making inferences from implied information.

With regard to understanding facts, recall for a moment Levin and Pressley's discussion of Gordon, Hansen, and Pearson's spider study (1978). The children who had previously learned about spiders remembered more from their reading than did children not having previous "spider" training.

Thus, filling in the gaps in one's schema leads to improved retention. Presenting content clarifying overviews, advance organizers, and pictures to children before they begin to read also provides schemata leading to better representation and retention of information (Levin and Pressley, this volume). Even though this is the case, it should be realized that these "content-clarifying" or "stage-setting" devices are optimal only when the material is moderately difficult to read (Pearson, this volume). If the material is easy for the child and the child already has a conceptually rich, well organized schema relevant to the passage, then additional author or teacher imposed schemata are superfluous. Moreover, if the other extreme exists and the material is too difficult or the child has little or no relevant schema, then such content clarifying preinstruction "will not take." Research psychologists are becoming aware of the need to take into account individual differences in regard to schema development and reading comprehension. Educators, I am sure, will welcome such individualistic concern.

In addition to providing a better understanding of the facts of a passage, schemata allow one to make inferences about missing information. As noted by Baker and Stein, children can draw inferences and there appears to be a developmental difference in that older children are better at drawing inferences than are younger children. Most work so far has been done with very simplistic stories and sentence triplets. Consequently, research is not yet at a point where it has much applicability to instructional settings. Yet, knowing that children can make inferences is a first step toward examining inferential thinking at higher levels of comprehension.

The story grammar research is a promising extension of schema theory. This body of research focuses on how people make use of their prior knowledge about stories to help understand new stories. Story grammars are not content specific, but instead are generalized ideas about the structure of stories developed through recurrent exposure to stories. Such structural knowledge helps a person understand the relationships of events and allows one to anticipate material.

While story grammars provide us with some help in understanding how certain knowledge is represented, activated, or inferred, they are presently modeled on very simple stories. Thus, their applicability is limited. Yet, they provide us with a beginning effort at understanding how one type of abstract prior knowledge may be brought to bear on new material. Story grammars may be extremely useful for operationalizing some important comprehension processes.

Understanding how background knowledge can be activated is, of course, an essential problem for teachers. In order for a teacher to guide a child toward independence in activating background knowledge, and in applying it to reading, the teacher must know if the child has the necessary concepts and world knowledge organized for retrieval. Hopefully, the current research on schema theory and story grammars will help in these efforts but, at present, there remains a large gap between the practical problems of teaching comprehension and the theoretical efforts of cognitive psychology.

Research to this point has done little more than verify teacher intuitions. Yet such verification is important for it provides teachers with the confidence to stress even more the development and activation of background knowledge. What we now need is to progress toward a more specific understanding of how background knowledge functions in particular reading situations. It is unlikely that work in cognitive psychology will, or even should, provide recipes for schema development and activation specific to particular pieces of information. However, it would be useful if cognitive psychologists would work with teachers to explore specific techniques for activating prior knowledge. Teachers now use a variety of methods, such as having students survey their text, brainstorm about concepts, do preliminary research on topics, or generate questions related to the topic. The impact of these techniques should be assessed, keeping in mind both the psychologist's explanations as to how such devices should work, and the educator's concern that conclusions be applicable to particular children reading specific material.

Main Ideas

The process of extracting main ideas from what we read has always received a great deal of attention in elementary classrooms. In the present volume, we find a similar interest in the abstraction of main ideas. Indeed, every author was concerned with this problem. Given all of this attention, one would hope that some simple summary statements might be made about the process of abstracting ideas. Unfortunately, this is not the case.

Baker and Stein present evidence indicating that children in both reading and listening tasks tend to remember important information more readily than unimportant information. Perhaps the most exciting aspect of this work is that there seems to be a developmental shift in what children perceive as important. Namely, children as young as first grade have consistent ideas about important aspects of a story, but their ideas are different from those of older children. As noted in the work of Stein and Glenn (1978), first graders focused more on consequences of actions, while fifth graders perceived the goals of character to be more important. The idea of a developmental shift in a child's concept of importance is a particularly interesting discovery given the propensity of both teachers and researchers to judge the quality of children's thought according to an adult view of the world.

With regard to main idea research, several cautionary remarks are warranted. Foremost is the fact that much of the research examining main ideas can be explained equally well without even using the concept of main idea (Trabasso, this volume). That is, sentences containing main ideas are more memorable than other sentences independent of their role in the passage. For example, Baker and Stein noted that an idea specified as important in the experimental materials were generally actions; whereas, those specified as less important were static descriptions. Furthermore, there is clear evidence in the developmental literature that actions totally devoid of surrounding text are more memorable than static descriptions. Thus, children and adults may remember main ideas best simply because they are the most memorable events.

Another problem, aptly described in both the Pearson and Johnson chapters, is the confusion surrounding the definition of "main idea." To borrow from Pearson, the "term main idea is but a 'main idea' for a polyglot of tasks and relationships among ideas." In most of the work reviewed by Baker and Stein, main ideas were perceived as the most important pieces of information in a paragraph or simple story but, as Pearson notes, there were other studies where main ideas were either the most general ideas or the most related to the overall theme of a passage. Pearson also remarked that there are situations where a main idea may fill all of these criteria, and other situations where a main idea may meet one or two of the criteria.

Part of the confusion in defining main ideas is the fact that the teaching model has a different criterion for specifying main points than does the psychological model of reading comprehension. For example, the psychological model is very tied to singular episodes of information; whereas, at times, the teaching model is also tied to specific episodes, but more often examines main ideas across multiple episodes. A typical teaching situation is to have children come up with their own titles to a story which, of course, requires the integration of ideas from many different sources within the story. Work in psychology has not yet moved beyond the representation of insular pieces of information. Again, we have the problem of a mismatch between the teaching and psychological models of concern with comprehension.

Yet important strides which should not be overlooked have been made in psychology. Educators should be aware of some analytic tools now available for text analysis. Recall for a moment Johnson and Barrett's classification of comprehension skills. While such taxonomies are extremely worthwhile, the analysis rests almost entirely on intuition. To avoid the problems inherent in an intuitive definition of comprehension skills, these skills must be more objectively defined. Trabasso felt that both propositional analysis and story grammars might serve this need. For example, Trabasso points to some recent work by Kintsch and Vipond (in press) where they used propositional analysis to come up with the most general and frequent ideas of a text. Such an approach may be a very good way to operationalize main ideas.

A better definition of reading skills, however, is just the first step in theory development (Trabasso, this volume). Also needed are descriptions of how children arrive at main points during reading.

As a good place to start, Marjorie Johnson suggested that we need more direct observation of children in classroom-like settings. Johnson warned that for any experimental or educational situations, care must be taken to insure that materials are both appropriate for the reader and appropriate to the task under examination. In this case, materials should be written so that reading for the main idea is a realistic motive and intrinsic to the structure and content of the material. Given the appropriate materials, the experimenter could then engage the reader in an introspective analysis of just what he or she did to extract main points from the material. After observing a sample of children, the researcher might begin formulating hypotheses regarding the thinking strategies children seem to use for extracting main points. These strategies could then be put to a more rigorous experimental test. In any case, experimenters need to begin examining issues, such as reading for the main idea, in situations where motivation demands, material demands, and task demands are more realistic (Johnson).

Finally, educators need answers to a myriad of specific questions concerning main ideas. For example, should main ideas be taught wholistically, or should the task be broken down into a smaller sequence of skills? Are main ideas located in the beginning of paragraphs easier for children to understand than those located in other positions? Should students have practice isolating main ideas in short selections before they are introduced to main ideas in longer selections? Are implied main ideas a higher level skill than explicit main ideas? In sum, does making students aware of how main ideas are structured and then developed help them with their comprehension?

Instructional Strategies

One area where considerable interchange has occurred between the educator and psychologist is that of instructional strategies. In fact, research has been particularly useful to the educator in corroborating teaching intuitions and in providing teachers with ideas for instruction. Most help in this area has come from what Levin and Pressley have described as prose-dependent strategies. Their summary of work in content clarifying (advance organizers, instructional objectives) and orienting tasks (pictures, themes) provided to students before they read have important educational implications, particularly for the publishers of texts (Pearson, this volume).

The same conclusion holds true for prose dependent strategies, used during the reading of text: pictures, typographical headings, marginal comments, embedded questions. Although this work must be expanded and refined, it is exciting to see that psychologists are embracing prose dependent instructional strategies as an important area of research.

Teachers should also be pleased that researchers are generating research in processor-dependent strategies—those which readers apply to facilitate their own comprehension. Our applied contributors to this volume (Dale Johnson, Thomas Barrett, and Marjorie Johnson) all mention the importance of children taking responsibility for their own comprehension. Levin and Pressley's discussion of such processor-dependent strategies as imagery and summarizing is in the spirit of bridging the gap between cognitive psychology and education.

Another way to bridge the gap would be to examine various processor-dependent strategies over a longer time frame to determine if particular strategies introduced in an experimental situation have any carryover to students' independent reading. Processor-dependent strategies that evolve into student initiated activities would have important educational implications.

Metacognition

Educators will undoubtedly welcome psychologists' recent interest in metacognition. Two important educational issues are being tested: the question of reader independence (or, more precisely, the lack of reader independence) and the role of critical thinking in comprehension. Both of these issues are intrinsic to an educational model of comprehension.

In regard to the independence-dependence question, researchers have discovered that young children are not as competent as older children in monitoring their own comprehension

(Baker, in press). Readers do not know when they do or do not understand because they, young children particularly, have little awareness of their own cognitive processing (Baker & Stein, this volume).

Lack of self-monitoring can also be a problem for the adult reader. Take, for example, a student of mine who had just flunked her last introductory psychology examination. She had the proper "good student facade"; she underlined essential points in her text and had an adequate set of lecture notes. She also claimed to spend a considerable amount of time studying. After having her reread a short selection from her psychology text, I was somewhat amazed that she could not even answer the simplest question. Thinking she might have a poor memory, I asked her several other questions allowing her to look back in her text for the appropriate answer. Still, she had no success. What is interesting is that she was very surprised that she had comprehended so little. She had assumed she had understood without ever testing her assumption and appeared totally oblivious to strategies which might help her monitor her comprehension. Unfortunately, I am afraid she is typical of many poor achieving college students. In sum, these students have failed to become independent readers.

My student corresponded to typical young children in not questioning their understanding or memory of information (Baker & Stein). Recall for a moment Baker and Stein's comments about how young school children could not tell why passages differed in difficulty and were unaware they had misunderstood directions (Markman, 1977). Markman also found that older children are better than younger children in detecting inconsistencies. Younger children were unaware that certain aspects of the text did not make any sense.

Teaching children to be critical of their own comprehension is now beginning to recieve some attention in research (see Baker, 1980, for a review). So far, the work has been similar to the above in being very content based where children and adults examine materials for inconsistencies. Yet, several conclusions have emerged from this work which should sound very familiar to educators.

To evaluate material for inconsistencies in style and content, children need to have a model or concept of a properly formed piece of writing. In other words, it is necessary for one to develop an internal standard of excellence which can only come about through many exposures to well written materials.

It is promising to note that Trabasso, Johnson, and Pearson were all very encouraged about what is now known about text writing. In fact, the state of the art is such that certain principles gleaned from research can be safely offered to publishers for creating more comprehensible and better written materials. For example, many of the prose dependent strategies specified by Levin and Pressley have direct applicability to publishers. Moreover, enough progress has been made regarding text structure (propositional analysis, story grammars) for us to know what aspects of structure lead to more comprehensible materials.

To help children comprehend better and create internal standards of excellence, beginning readers should only be exposed to well structured material where relationships inherent in the text are well specified (Pearson). Children should experience paragraphs which logically build toward main points and essential points should at first be clearly marked by the author. After children have developed a standard of excellence they can begin evaluating materials which may or may not match up to their internal standards.

Finally, the metacognition literature brings to the forefront the issue of developing reader independence. In order to develop adequate comprehension abilities, it is crucial that children learn to "know what they know." Otherwise, children will constantly depend upon some external source (usually the teacher) to gauge themselves and their efforts.

This conclusion brings to mind some comments made by Marjorie Johnson when she noted that too often purposes for reading are established for the child by the teacher. Teachers, instead, should lead children toward establishing their own motives for reading and then allow them to judge for themselves whether they have met their reading objectives. The children should then have an opportunity to relate how they solved their purpose. Providing many such opportunities for self-monitoring should help children become self-questioning, independent readers. To do this, many teachers will have to change their instructional style to guide rather than direct the monitoring process.

Conclusion

It seems as if we have indeed made a good start in understanding children's reading comprehension. We have seen a shift in focus of psychology in the direction of relevance, and educators are becoming increasingly receptive to the ideas and issues psychologists are beginning to raise.

As has become so apparent throughout this volume, a psychological understanding of comprehension is far from complete. Real progress has been made but, for progress to continue, psychologists need to expand and make specific their models to incorporate the many problems apparent to educators. In spite of the obvious shortcomings, psychology does offer something important to the educator; namely, the beginning of a theoretical philosophy or approach to instruction grounded on an empirical base. Educators too often choose a specific task or technique based only on intuition or habit. Such choices should be guided not only by specific psychological research, which is often lacking, but also by the more general ideas about comprehension that are by now well documented by psychological research.

On the other hand, the present volume makes it apparent that the educator can offer much to the psychologist. Educators' wealth of experience and concern with teaching comprehension have made them well aware of specific issues and problems that must be understood. The experienced reading teacher can provide a test of sufficiency against which models of reading comprehension can be evaluated and revised.

Our conclusions make apparent the need for an interdisciplinary approach to understanding what comprehension is and how it should be taught.

References

ANDERSON, C.J., and I. DAVIDSON. *Reading Objectives*. New York. Laurel Book, 1933.

ANDERSON, R.C. "How to Construct Achievement Tests to Assess Comprehension," *Review of Educational Research*, 42 (1972), 145–170.

ANDERSON, R.C. "The Notion of Schemata and the Educational Enterprise," in R.C. Anderson, R.J. Spiro, and W.E. Montague (Eds.), *Schooling and the Acquisition of Knowledge*. Hillsdale, New Jersey: Erlbaum, 1977.

ANDERSON, R.C., and W.B. BIDDLE. "On Asking People Questions About What They Are Reading," in G. Bower (Ed.), *The Psychology of Learning and Motivation* (Volume 9). New York: Academic Press, 1975.

ANDERSON, R.C., R.E. REYNOLDS, D.L. SCHALLERT, and E.T. GOETZ. "Frameworks for Comprehending Discourse," *American Educational Research Journal*, 14 (1977), 367–381.

ANDERSON, R.C., R.J. SPIRO, and W.E. MONTAGUE (Eds.). *Schooling and the Acquisition of Knowledge*. Hillsdale, New Jersey: Erlbaum, 1977.

ANDERSON, T.H. "Study Strategies and Adjunct Aids," in R.J. Spiro, B.C. Bruce, and W.F. Brewer (Eds.), *Theoretical Issues in Reading Comprehension: Perspectives from Cognitive Psychology, Linguistics, Artificial Intelligence, and Education*. Hillsdale, New Jersey, Erlbaum, 1980.

ANDRICH, D., and J.R. GODFREY. "Hierarchies in the Skills of Davis' *Reading Comprehension Test, Form D:* An Empirical Investigation Using a Latent Trait Model," *Reading Research Quarterly*, 14 (1978–1979), 182–200.

ARNOLD, D.J., and P.H. BROOKS. "Influence of Contextual Organizing Material on Children's Listening Comprehension," *Journal of Educational Psychology*, 68 (1976), 711–716.

ARTLEY, A.S. "Statistical Analysis of the Relationship between General Reading Comprehension and Comprehension in a Specific Subject Matter Area," doctoral dissertation, Pennsylvania State College, 1942.

AUSUBEL, D.P. *The Psychology of Meaningful Verbal Learning.* New York: Grune and Stratton, 1963.

BAKER, L. "Knowing When We Don't Understand (and What to Do about It)," in P.D. Pearson, *What's New in Reading?* Clinic presented at the meeting of the American Association of School Administrators, Minneapolis, July 1978.

BAKER, L. "Processing Temporal Relationships in Simple Stories: Effects of Input Sequence," *Journal of Verbal Learning and Verbal Behavior,* 17 (1978), 559–572.

BAKER, L. *Do I Understand or Do I Not Understand? That Is the Question.* Reading Education Report No. 10. Champaign, Illinois: Center for the Study of Reading, 1979.

BAKER, L., and J.L. SANTA. "Context, Integration, and Retrieval," *Memory and Cognition,* 5 (1977), 308–314.

BAKER, L., J.L. SANTA, and J.M. GENTRY. "Consequences of Rigid and Flexible Learning," *Bulletin of the Psychonomic Society,* 9 (1977), 58–60.

BARNES, B.R., and E.U. CLAWSON. "Do Advance Organizers Facilitate Learning? Recommendations for Further Research Based on an Analysis of 32 Studies," *Review of Educational Research,* 45 (1975), 637–659.

BARTLETT, F.C. *Remembering: A Study in Experimental and Social Psychology.* Cambridge, England: Cambridge University Press, 1932.

BEDELL, R.C. *Relationship between the Ability to Recall and the Ability to Infer in Specific Learning Situations.* Bulletin 34, No. 9. Kirksville, Missouri: Northeast Missouri State Teachers College, 1934.

BENDER, B.G., and J.R. LEVIN. "Pictures, Imagery, and Retarded Children's Prose Learning," *Journal of Educational Psychology,* 20 (1978), 583–588.

BETTS, E.A. *Foundations of Reading Instruction.* New York: American Book, 1957.

BINET, A., and V. HENRI. "La memoire des phrases (memoire des idees)," *L'annee Psychologique,* 1 (1894), 24–59.

BLANK, M., and S.M. FRANK. "Story Recall in Kindergarten Children: Effects of Method of Presentation on Psycholinguistic Performance," *Child Development,* 42 (1971), 299–312.

BLOOM, S. *Taxonomy of Educational Objectives Handbook I: Cognitive Domain.* New York: David McKay, 1956.

BOND, E. "Reading and Ninth Grade Achievements," *Teachers College Contributions to Education,* No. 756. New York: Columbia University, 1938.

BORMUTH, J.R., et al. "Children's Comprehension of between- and Within-Sentence Syntactic Structures," *Journal of Educational Psychology,* 61 (1970), 349–357.

BOTVIN, G.J., and B. SUTTON-SMITH. "The Development of Structural Complexity in Children's Fantasy Narratives," *Developmental Psychology,* 13 (1977), 377–388.

BOWER, G.H. "Experiments on Story Understanding and Recall," *Quarterly Journal of Experimental Psychology,* 28 (1976), 511–534.

BRANSFORD, J.D., J.R. BARCLAY, and J.J. FRANKS. "Sentence Memory: A Constructive versus Interpretive Approach," *Cognitive Psychology,* 3 (1972), 193–209.

BRANSFORD, J.D., and M.K. JOHNSON. "Contextual Prerequisites for Understanding: Some Investigations of Comprehension and Recall," *Journal of Verbal Learning and Verbal Behavior,* 11 (1972), 717–726.

BRANSFORD, J.D., and M.K. JOHNSON. "Considerations of Some Problems of Comprehension," in W.G. Chase (Ed.), *Visual Information Processing.* New York: Academic Press, 1973.

BRANSFORD, J.D., and N.S. McCARRELL. "A Sketch of a Cognitive Approach to Comprehension: Some Thoughts about Understanding What it Means to Comprehend," in D. Palermo and W. Weimer (Eds.), *Cognition and the Symbolic Processes.* Hillsdale, New Jersey: Erlbaum, 1974.

BROWN, A.L. "Recognition, Reconstruction and Recall of Narrative Sequences by Preoperational Children," *Child Development,* 46 (1975a), 156–166.

BROWN, A.L. "The Development of Memory: Knowing, Knowing about Knowing, and Knowing How to Know," in H.W. Reese (Ed.), *Advances in Child Development and Behavior* (Volume 10). New York: Academic Press, 1975b.

BROWN, A.L. "The Construction of Temporal Succession by Preoperational Children," in A.D. Pick (Ed.), *Minnesota Symposium on Child Psychology* (Volume 10). Minneapolis: University of Minnesota, 1976a.

BROWN, A.L. "Semantic Integration in Children's Reconstruction of Narrative Sequences," *Cognitive Psychology,* 8 (1976b), 247–262.

BROWN, A.L. "Metacognitive Development and Reading," in R.J. Spiro, B. Bruce, and W. Brewer (Eds.), *Theoretical Issues in Reading Comprehension.* Hillsdale, New Jersey: Erlbaum, in press.

BROWN, A.L., and M.D. MURPHY. "Reconstruction of Arbitrary versus Logical Sequences By Preschool Children," *Journal of Experimental Child Psychology,* 20 (1975), 307–326.

BROWN, A.L., and S.S. SMILEY. "The Development of Strategies for Studying Texts," *Child Development,* 49 (1978), 1076–1088.

BROWN, A.L., and S.S. SMILEY. "Rating the Importance of Structural Units of Prose Passages: A Problem of Metacognitive Development," *Child Development,* 48 (1977), 1–8.

BROWNING, W.G. "A Critical Review of Research and Expert Opinion on the Underlining Study Aid," in W.D. Miller and G.H. McNinch (Eds.), *Reflections and Investigations on Reading,* Twenty-Fifth National Reading Conference Yearbook. Clemson, South Carolina: National Reading Conference, 1976.

BRUCE, B. "What Makes a Good Story?" *Language Arts,* 55 (1978), 460–466.

References

BRUNER, J., J. GOODNOW, and G. AUSTIN. *A Study of Thinking.* New York: John Wiley and Sons, 1956.

CARROLL, J.B. *Learning from Verbal Discourse in Educational Media: A Review of the Literature.* Research Bulletin No. 71-61. Princeton, New Jersey: Educational Testing Service, 1971.

CARROLL, J.B. "Defining Language Comprehension: Some Speculations," in J.B. Carroll and R.O. Freedle (Eds.), *Language Comprehension and the Acquisition of Knowledge.* Washington, D.C.: Winston, 1972.

CARROLL, R.P. "An Experimental Study of Comprehension in Reading, with Special Reference to the Reading of Directions," doctoral dissertation, Teachers College, Columbia University, 1926.

CHASE, W.G., and H.H. CLARK. "Mental Operations in the Comparison of Sentences and Pictures," in L.W. Gredd (Ed.), *Cognition in Learning and Memory.* New York: John Wiley and Sons, 1972.

CHI, M.T.H. "Knowledge Structures and Memory Development," in R.S. Siegler (Ed.), *Children's Thinking: What Develops?* Hillsdale, New Jersey: Erlbaum, 1978.

CHRISTIE, D.J., and G.M. SCHUMACHER. "Developmental Trends in the Abstraction and Recall of Relevant versus Irrelevant Thematic Information from Connected Verbal Materials," *Child Development,* 46 (1975), 598–602.

CLARK, E.V. "On the Acquisition of the Meaning of 'Before' and 'After'," *Journal of Verbal Learning and Verbal Behavior,* 10 (1971), 266–275.

CLARK, H.H. "Bridging," in R.C. Schank and B.L. Nash-Webber, *Theoretical Issues in Natural Language Processing.* Cambridge, Massachusetts, 1975.

CLARK, H.H., and E.V. CLARK. "Semantic Distinctions and Memory for Complex Sentences," *Quarterly Journal of Experimental Psychology,* 20 (1968), 129–138.

COLBY, B., and M. COLE. "Culture, Memory, and Narrative," in R. Horton and R. Finnegan (Eds.), *Modes of Thought: Essays on Thinking in Western and Non-Western Societies.* London: Faber and Faber, 1973.

COLLINS, A. "Processes in Acquiring and Using Knowledge," in R.C. Anderson, R.J. Spiro, and W.E. Montague (Eds.), *Schooling and the Acquisition of Knowledge.* Hillsdale, New Jersey: Erlbaum, 1977, 339–363.

COOMBS, C.H., R.M. DAWES, and A. TVERSKY. *Mathematical Psychology: An Elementary Introduction.* Englewood Cliffs, New Jersey: Prentice-Hall, 1970.

CRAIK, F.I.M., and R.S. LOCKHART. "Levels of Processing: A Framework for Memory Research," *Journal of Verbal Learning and Verbal Behavior,* 11 (1972), 671–684.

CROTHERS, E.J. "Memory Structure and the Recall of Discourse," in J.B. Carroll and R.O. Freedle (Eds.), *Language Comprehension and the Acquisition of Knowledge.* Washington, D.C.: Winston, 1972.

DAHLBERG, L.A. "Children's Comprehension of Pronoun-Antecedent Relations in Connected Discourse," master's thesis, University of Wisconsin at Madison, 1978.

DANNER, F.W. "Children's Understanding of Intersentence Organization in the Recall of Short Descriptive Passages," *Journal of Educational Psychology*, 68 (1976), 174–183.

DANSEREAU, D.F., B.A. McDONALD, K.W. COLLINS, J. GARLAND, C.D. HOLLEY, G. DICKHOFF, and S.H. EVANS. "Evaluation of a Learning Strategy System," in H.F. O'Neill, Jr. and C.D. Spielberger (Eds.), *Cognitive and Affective Learning Strategies*. New York: Academic Press, 1979.

DAVIDSON, R.E. "The Role of Metaphor and Analogy in Learning," in J.R. Levin and V.L. Allen (Eds.), *Cognitive Learning in Children: Theories and Strategies*. New York: Academic Press, 1976.

DAVIS, F.B. "Fundamental Factors of Comprehension in Reading," *Psychometrika*, 9 (1944), 185–197.

DAVIS, F.B. "Research in Comprehension in Reading," *Reading Research Quarterly*, 3 (1968), 499–545.

DAVIS, F.B. "Psychometric Research on Comprehension in Reading," *Reading Research Quarterly*, 7 (1972), 628–678.

DAWES, R.M. "Memory and Distortion of Meaningful Written Materials," *British Journal of Psychology*, 57 (1966), 77–86.

DECHANT, E.V. *Improving the Teaching of Reading*. Englewood Cliffs, New Jersey: Prentice-Hall, 1970.

DEE-LUCAS, D., and F.J. DiVESTA. "Learner-Generated Organizational Aids: Effects on Learning from Text," *Journal of Educational Psychology*, 72 (1980), 304–311.

DEUTSCHE, J.M. *The Development of Children's Concepts of Causal Relations*. University of Minnesota Institute of Child Welfare Monograph, 1937.

DEWEY, J.C. "The Acquisition of Facts as a Measure of Reading Comprehension," *Elementary School Journal*, 35 (January 1935), 346–348.

DOCTOROW, M., M.C. WITTROCK, and C. MARKS. "Generative Processes in Reading Comprehension," *Journal of Educational Psychology*, 70 (1978), 109–118.

DONALDSON, M., and G. BALFOR. "Less is More: A Study of Language Comprehension in Children," *British Journal of Psychology*, 59 (1968), 461–471.

DUNHAM, T.C., and J.R. LEVIN. "Imagery Instructions and Young Children's Prose Learning: No Evidence of 'Support'," *Contemporary Educational Psychology*, 4 (1979), 107–113.

DURKIN, D. *What Classroom Observations Reveal about Reading Comprehension Instruction*. Technical Report No. 106. Urbana, Illinois: Center for the Study of Reading, University of Illinois, October 1978. Eric Document No. ED 162 259.

FARR, R. *Reading: What Can Be Measured?* Newark, Delaware: International Reading Association, 1969.

FEDER, D.D. "Comprehension Maturity Tests: A New Technique in Mental Measurement," *Journal of Educational Psychology,* 29 (1938), 597–606.

FISCHER, J.A. "Effects of a Cue Synthesis Procedure and Postquestions on the Retention of Prose Material," *Dissertation Abstracts International,* 34 (1973), 615.

FLAPPAN, D. *Children's Understanding of Social Interaction.* New York: Teachers College Press, 1968.

FLAVELL, J.H. "Metacognitive Development," in J.M. Scandura and C.J. Brainerd (Eds.), *Structural/Process Theories of Complex Human Behavior.* Alphen a.d. Rijn, The Netherlands: Sijthoff and Noordhoff, 1978.

FLAVELL, J.H., and H.M. WELLMAN. "Metamemory," in R.V. Kail, Jr. and J.W. Hagan (Eds.), *Perspectives on the Development of Memory and Cognition.* Hillsdale, New Jersey: Erlbaum, 1977.

FRASE, L.T. "Boundary Conditions for Mathemagenic Behaviors," *Review of Educational Research,* 40 (1970), 337–347.

FRASE, L.T. "Prose Processing," in G. Bower (Ed.), *Psychology of Learning and Motivation.* New York: Academic Press, 1975.

FRASE, L.T. "Typographical Supports for Reading Comprehension," paper presented at the annual meeting of the American Psychological Association, San Francisco, August 1977.

FREDERICKSON, C.H. "Effects of Task-Induced Cognitive Operations on Comprehension and Memory Processes," in J.B. Carroll and R.O. Freedle (Eds.), *Language Comprehension and the Acquisition of Knowledge.* Washington, D.C.: Winston, 1972.

FRENCH, L.A., and A.L. BROWN. "Comprehension of before and after in Logical and Arbitrary Sequences," *Journal of Child Language,* 3 (1976), 247–256.

GAGNE, E.D. "Long Term Retention of Information Following Learning from Prose," *Review of Educational Research,* 48 (1978), 629–665.

GANS, R. "A Study of Critical Reading Comprehension in the Intermediate Grades," *Teachers College Contributions to Education,* No. 811, 1940.

GERHARD, C. *Making Sense: Reading Comprehension Improved through Categorizing.* Newark, Delaware: International Reading Association, 1975.

GLASS, A., K. HOLYOAK, and J. SANTA. *Cognition.* Reading, Massachusetts: Addison-Wesley, 1979.

GLENN, C.G. "The Role of Episodic Structure and of Story Length in Children's Recall of Simple Stories," *Journal of Verbal Learning and Verbal Behavior,* 17 (1978), 229–247.

GOETZ, E., and B. ARMBRUSTER. "Psychological Correlates of Text Structure," in R. Spiro, B. Bruce, and W. Brewer (Eds.), *Theoretical Issues in Reading Comprehension.* Hillsdale, New Jersey: Erlbaum, in press.

GOLDSTEIN, K., and M. SCHEERER. "Abstract and Concrete Behavior: An Experimental Study with Special Tests," *Psychological Monographs,* #239, 55 (1941).

GOLDSTEIN, H. "Reading and Listening Comprehension at Various Controlled Rates," unpublished doctoral dissertation, Teachers College, Columbia University, New York, 1940.

GOMULICKI, B.R. "Recall As an Abstractive Process," *Acta Psychologica,* 12 (1956), 77–94.

GOODMAN, K.S. "A Linguistic Study of Cues and Miscues in Reading," *Elementary English,* 42 (1965), 639–643.

GOODMAN, K.S., and Y. GOODMAN. "Learning about Psycholinguistic Processes by Analyzing Oral Reading," *Harvard Education Review,* 47 (1977), 317–333.

GORDON, C., J. HANSEN, and P.D. PEARSON. *"Effect of Background Knowledge on Silent Reading Comprehension,"* paper presented at the annual meeting of the American Educational Research Association, Toronto, March 1978.

GRAY, W.S. "Principles of Method in Teaching Reading as Derived from Scientific Investigation," *National Society for the Study of Education, Eighteenth Yearbook,* Part II. Bloomington, Illinois: Public School Publishing Company, 1919, 26–51.

GREENO, J.G. "Process of Understanding in Problem Solving," in N.J. Castellan, Jr., D.B. Pisoni, and G.R. Potts (Eds.), *Cognitive Theory* (Volume 2). Hillsdale, New Jersey: Erlbaum, 1977.

GRICE, H.P. "Logic and Conversation," in P. Cole and J.L. Morgan (Eds.), *Syntax and Semantics: Speech Acts* (Volume 3). New York: Academic Press, 1975.

GRIESE, ARNOLD A. *Do You Read Me? Practical Approaches to Teaching Reading Comprehension.* Santa Monica, California: Goodyear, 1977.

GRUENEICH, R. "Children's Use of Intention and Consequence Information in Making Evaluative Inferences," unpublished doctoral thesis, University of Minnesota, 1978.

GUSZAK, F.J. "Reading: Comprehension Skills," in P. Lamb and R. Arnold (Eds.), *Reading: Foundations and Instructional Strategies.* Belmont, California: Wadsworth, 1976.

GUSZAK, F.J. "Teacher Questioning and Reading," *Reading Teacher,* 21 (1967), 227–234.

GUTTMANN, J., J.R. LEVIN, and M. PRESSLEY. "Pictures, Partial Pictures, and Young Children's Oral Prose Learning," *Journal of Educational Psychology,* 69 (1977), 473–480.

HALL, W.E., and F.P. ROBINSON. "An Analytical Approach to the Study of Reading Skills," *Journal of Educational Psychology,* 36 (1945), 429–442.

HARTLEY, J., and I.K. DAVIES. "Preinstructional Strategies: The Role of Pretests, Behavioral Objectives, Overviews, and Advance Organizers," *Review of Educational Research,* 46 (1976), 239–265.

HAWKINS, P.D. "Hypostatization of Selected Environmental Concepts in Elementary School Children," unpublished master's thesis, University of Wisconsin, 1971.

HITTLEMAN, D.R. *Developmental Reading: A Psycholinguistic Perspective.* Chicago: Rand McNally, 1978.

HOMZIE, M.J., and C.B. GRAVITT. "Children's Reproduction: Effects of Event Order and Implied versus Directly Stated Causation," *Journal of Child Language,* 3 (1976), 237–246.

HOOD, J. "Qualitative Analysis of Oral Reading Errors: The Interjudge Reliability of Scores," *Reading Research Quarterly,* 11 (1975–1976), 577–598.

IRION, T. "Comprehension Difficulties of Ninth Grade Students in the Study of Literature," unpublished doctoral dissertation, Teachers College, Columbia University, 1925.

JOHNSON, D.D., and T.C. BARRETT. This volume.

JOHNSON, D.D., and P.D. PEARSON. *Teaching Reading Vocabulary.* New York: Holt, Rinehart and Winston, 1978.

JOHNSON, M.K., J.D. BRANSFORD, S.E. NYBERG, and J.J. CLEARY. "Comprehension Factors in Interpreting Memory for Abstract and Concrete Sentences," *Journal of Verbal Learning and Verbal Behavior,* 11 (1972), 451–454.

JOHNSON, R.E. "Recall of Prose as a Function of the Structural Importance of the Linguistic Units," *Journal of Verbal Learning and Verbal Behavior,* 9 (1970), 12–20.

JOHNSON, R.E. "Abstractive Processes in the Remembering of Prose," *Journal of Educational Psychology,* 66 (1974), 772–779.

KAIL, R.V., M.T.H. CHI, A.L. INGRAM, and F.W. DANNER. "Constructive Aspects of Children's Reading Comprehension," *Child Development,* 48 (1977), 684–688.

KINTSCH, W. *The Representation of Meaning in Memory.* Hillsdale, New Jersey: Erlbaum, 1974.

KINTSCH, W., and D. VIPOND. "Reading Comprehension and Readability in Educational Practice and Psychological Theory," in L.G. Nilsson (Ed.), *Memory Processes.* Hillsdale, New Jersey: Erlbaum, in press.

KOHLBERG, L. "Stage and Sequence: The Cognitive-Developmental Approach to Socialization," in D.A. Goslin (Ed.), *Handbook of Socialization Theory and Research.* New York: Rand McNally, 1969.

KULHAVY, R.W. "Feedback in Written Instruction," *Review of Educational Research,* 47 (1977), 211–232.

LADAS, H. "The Mathemagenic Effects of Factual Review Questions on the Learning of Incidental Information: A Critical Review," *Review of Educational Research,* 43 (1973), 71–82.

LAMB, P., and R. ARNOLD. *Reading: Foundations and Instructional Strategies.* Belmont, California: Wadsworth, 1976.

LANE, J., and J.J. ANDERSON. "Integration of Intention and Outcome in Moral Judgment," *Memory and Cognition,* 4 (1976), 1–5.

LANGSAUN, R.S. "A Factorial Analysis of Reading Ability," *Journal of Experimental Education,* 10 (1941), 57–63.

LAPP, D., and J. FLOOD. *Teaching Reading to Every Child.* New York: Macmillan, 1978.

LAWTON, J.T., and S.K. WANSKA. "Advance Organizers as a Teaching Strategy: A Reply to Barnes and Clawson," *Review of Educational Research,* 47 (1977), 233–244.

LEHNERT, W. "Human and Computational Question Answering," *Cognitive Science,* 1 (1977), 47–73.

LEONDAR, B. "Hatching Plots: Genesis of Storymaking," in D. Perkins and B. Leondar (Eds.), *The Arts and Cognition.* Baltimore: Johns Hopkins, 1977.

LESGOLD, A.M., C. McCORMICK, and R.M. GOLINKOFF. "Imagery Training and Children's Prose Learning," *Journal of Educational Psychology,* 67 (1975), 663–667.

LEVI-STRAUSS, C. "The Structural Study of Myth," in T.A. Sebeok (Ed.), *Myth: A Symposium.* Bloomington: Indiana University Press, 1955.

LEVIN, J.R. "Comprehending What We Read: An Outsider Looks In," *Journal of Reading Behavior,* 4 (1972). 18–28.

LEVIN, J.R. "What Have We Learned about Maximizing What Children Learn?" in J.R. Levin and V.L. Allen (Eds.), *Cognitive Learning in Children: Theories and Strategies.* New York: Academic Press, 1976.

LEVIN, J.R. "Cognitive Strategies in Learning from Text," paper presented at the annual meeting of the American Educational Research Association, Toronto, March 1978.

LEVIN, J.R. "On Functions of Pictures in Prose," in F.J. Pirrozzolo and M.C. Wittrock (Eds.), *Neuropsychological and Cognitive Processes in Reading.* New York: Academic Press, in press.

LEVIN, J.R., B.G. BENDER, and A.M. LESGOLD. "Pictures, Repetition, and Young Children's Oral Prose Learning," *AV Communication Review,* 24 (1976), 367–380.

LEVIN, J.R., and A.M. LESGOLD. "On Pictures in Prose," *Educational Communication and Technology,* 26 (1978), 233–243.

MANDLER, J.M. "A Code in the Node: The Use of a Story Schema in Retrieval," *Discourse Processes,* 1 (1978), 14–35.

MANDLER, J.M., and N.S. JOHNSON. "Remembrance of Things Parsed: Story Structure and Recall," *Cognitive Psychology,* 9 (1977), 111–151.

MANEY, E.S. "Literal and Critical Reading in Science," unpublished doctoral dissertation, Temple University, 1952.

MARKMAN, E.M. "Realizing that You Don't Understand: A Preliminary Investigation," *Child Development,* 48 (1977), 986–992.

MARSHALL, N., and M.D. GLOCK. "Comprehension of Connected Discourse: A Study into the Relationships between the Structure of Text and Information Recalled," *Reading Research Quarterly,* 14 (1978–1979), 10–56.

References   179

MEYER, B.J. *The Organization of Prose and Its Effect on Memory*. Amsterdam: North Holland, 1975.

MONTGOMERY COUNTY PUBLIC SCHOOLS. "Comprehension, Critical Reading, and Thinking Skills, K–12," *Teaching Reading Skills* (Volume 2), Bulletin No. 246. Rockville, Maryland: 1974.

NEILSON, A. "The Role of Macrostructures and Relational Markers in Comprehending Familiar and Unfamiliar Written Discourse," unpublished doctoral dissertation, University of Minnesota, 1977.

NEZWORSKI, T.M., N.L. STEIN, and T. TRABASSO. "Story Structure versus Content Effects on Children's Recall and Evaluative Inferences," paper presented at the Nineteenth Annual Meeting, Psychonomic Society, San Antonio, Texas, November 1978.

NICHOLAS, D.W., and T. TRABASSO. "Toward a Taxonomy of Inferences," in F. Wilkening and J. Becker (Eds.), *Information Integration by Children*. Hillsdale, New Jersey: Erlbaum, in press.

OMANSON, R.C. "The Event Analysis: A Methodology for the Empirical Study of Narrative Comprehension," unpublished paper, Institute of Child Development, University of Minnesota, 1978.

OMANSON, R.C., W.H. WARREN, and T. TRABASSO. "Goals, Themes, Inferences, and Memory: A Developmental Study," *Discourse Processing,* in press.

OTTO, W., R. CHESTER, J. McNEIL, and S. MEYERS. *Focused Reading Instruction*. Reading, Massachusetts: Addison-Wesley, 1974.

OTTO, W., T.C. BARRETT, and K. KOENKE. "Assessment of Children's Statements of the Main Idea in Reading," in J.A. Figurel (Ed.), *Reading and Realism*. Newark, Delaware: International Reading Association, 1969, 692–697.

PAIVIO, A. *Imagery and Verbal Processes*. New York: Holt, 1971.

PALERMO, D. "More about Less: A Study of Language Comprehension," *Journal of Verbal Learning and Verbal Behavior,* 12 (1973), 211–221.

PARIS, S.G. "Integration and Inference in Children's Comprehension and Memory," in F. Restle, R.M. Shiffrin, N.J. Castellan, H.R. Lindman, and D.B. Pisoni (Eds.), *Cognitive Theory* (Volume 1). Hillsdale, New Jersey: Erlbaum, 1975.

PARIS, S.G., and A.Y. CARTER. "Semantic and Constructive Aspects of Sentence Memory in Children," *Developmental Psychology,* 9 (1973), 109–113.

PARIS, S.G., and B.K. LINDAUER. "Constructive Aspects of Children's Comprehension and Memory," in R.V. Kail, Jr., and J.W. Hagen (Eds.), *Perspectives on the Development of Memory and Cognition*. Hillsdale, New Jersey: Erlbaum, 1977.

PARIS, S.G., and G.J. MAHONEY. "Cognitive Integration in Children's Memory for Sentences and Pictures," *Child Development,* 45 (1974), 633–642.

PARIS, S.G., and L.R. UPTON. "Children's Memory for Inferential Relationships in Prose," *Child Development,* 47 (1976), 660–668.

PEARSON, P.D., and J. HANSEN. "A Recent History of Developmental Reading," unpublished paper, University of Minnesota, 1978.

PEARSON, P.D., and D.D. JOHNSON. *Teaching Reading Comprehension*. New York: Holt, Rinehart and Winston, 1978.

PENG, C.Y., and J.R. LEVIN. "Pictures and Children's Story Recall: Some Questions of Durability," *Educational Communication and Technology*, 27 (1979), 89–95.

PIAGET, J. *The Language and Thought of the Child*. New York: Harcourt Brace Jovanovich, 1926.

PIAGET, J. *The Child's Conception of Physical Causality*. New York: Harcourt Brace Jovanovich, 1929.

PIAGET, J. *The Origins of Intelligence*. New York: International University Press, 1952.

PIO, C., and T. ANDRE. "Paraphrasing Highlighted Statements and Learning from Prose," paper presented at the annual meeting of the American Educational Research Association, New York, April 1977.

POULSON, D., E. KINTSCH, W. KINTSCH, and D. PREMACK. "Children's Comprehension and Memory for Stories," *Journal of Experimental Child Psychology*, in press.

PRESSLEY, G.M. "Mental Imagery Helps Eight Year Olds Remember What They Read," *Journal of Educational Psychology*, 68 (1976), 355–359.

PRESSLEY, M. "Imagery and Children's Learning: Putting the Picture in Developmental Perspective," *Review of Educational Research*, 47 (1977), 582–622.

PRINCE, G. *A Grammar of Stories*. The Hague: Mouton, 1973.

PROPP, V. *Morphology of the Folktale* (Volume 10). Bloomington, Indiana: University Research Center in Anthropology, Folklore, and Linguistics, 1958.

REDER, L.M. "The Role of Elaboration in the Comprehension and Retention of Prose: A Critical Review," *Review of Educational Research*, 50 (1980), 5–53.

REST, J.R. "New Approaches in the Assessment of Moral Judgment," in T. Lackonna (Ed.), *Moral Development and Behavior: Theory, Research, and Social Issues*. New York: Holt, Rinehart and Winston, 1976.

RICHARDS, I.A. *Practical Criticism*. New York: Harcourt Brace Jovanovich, 1929.

RICHEK, M.A. "Reading Comprehension of Anaphoric Forms in Varying Linguistic Contexts," *Reading Research Quarterly*, 12 (1976–1977), 145–165.

RICHMOND, M.G. "The Relationship of the Uniqueness of Prose Passages to the Effect of Question Placement and Question Relevance on the Acquisition and Retention of Information," in W.D. Miller and G.H. McNinch (Eds.), *Reflections and Investigations on Reading*, Twenty-Fifth National Reading Conference Yearbook. Clemson, South Carolina: National Reading Conference, 1976.

RIDING, R.J., and J.M. SHORE. "A Comparison of Two Methods of Improving Prose Comprehension in Educationally Subnormal Children," *British Journal of Educational Psychology*, 44 (1974), 300–303.

References   181

ROBINSON, F.P. *Effective Study* (revised edition). New York: Harper and Row, 1961.

ROHWER, W.D., JR. "Elaboration and Learning in Childhood and Adolescence," in H.W. Reese (Ed.), *Advances in Child Development and Behavior.* New York: Academic Press, 1973.

ROTHKOPF, E.Z. "The Concept of Mathemagenic Activities," *Review of Educational Research,* 40 (1970), 325–336.

ROTHKOPF, E.Z. "Structural Text Features and the Control of Processes in Learning from Written Materials," in R.O. Freedle and J.B. Carroll (Eds.), *Language Comprehension and the Acquisition of Knowledge.* Washington, D.C.: Winston, 1972.

ROWLS, M.D. "The Facilitative and Interactive Effects of Adjunct Questions on Retention of Eighth Graders across Three Prose Passages: Dissertation in Prose Learning," *Journal of Educational Psychology,* 68 (1976), 205–209.

ROYER, J.M., and G.W. CABLE. "Illustrations, Analogies, and Facilitative Transfer in Prose Learning," *Journal of Educational Psychology,* 68 (1976), 205–209.

ROYER, J.M., and D.J. CUNNINGHAM. *On the Theory and Measurement of Reading Comprehension,* Technical Report No. 91. Champaign: University of Illinois, Center for the Study of Reading, 1978.

RUCH, M.D., and J.R. LEVIN. "Pictorial Organization versus Verbal Repetition of Children's Prose: Evidence for Processing Differences," *AV Communication Review,* 25 (1977), 269–280.

RUCH, M.D., and J.R. LEVIN. "Partial Pictures as Imagery: Retrieval Cues in Young Children's Prose Recall," *Journal of Experimental Child Psychology,* 28 (1979), 268–279.

RUDDELL, R.B. *Reading-Language Instruction: Innovative Practices.* Englewood Cliffs, New Jersey: Prentice-Hall, 1974.

RUMELHART, D.E. "Notes on a Schema for Stories," in D.G. Bobrow and A. Collins (Eds.), *Representation and Understanding: Studies in Cognitive Science.* New York: Academic Press, 1975.

RUMELHART, D.E. *Toward an Interactive Model of Reading,* Technical Report No. 56. San Diego: Center for Human Information Processing, University of California, 1976.

RUMELHART, D.E., and A. ORTONY. "The Representation of Knowledge in Memory," in R.C. Anderson, R.J. Spiro, and W.E. Montague (Eds.), *Schooling and the Acquisition of Knowledge.* Hillsdale, New Jersey: Erlbaum, 1977.

SANDERS, N.M. *Classroom Questions.* New York: Harper and Row, 1966.

SCHACHTER, S. "An Investigation of the Effects of Vocabulary Instruction and Schemata Orientation upon Reading Comprehension," unpublished doctoral dissertation, University of Minnesota, 1978.

SCHALLERT, D.L. "The Role of Illustrations in Reading Comprehension," in R.J. Spiro, B.C. Bruce, and W.F. Brewer (Eds.), *Theoretical Issues in Reading Comprehension: Perspectives from Cognitive Psychology, Linguistics, Artificial Intelligence, and Education.* Hillsdale, New Jersey: Erlbaum, 1980.

SCHALLERT, D.L., G.M. KLEIMAN, and A.D. RUBIN. *Analysis of Differences between Oral and Written Language,* Technical Report No. 29. Champaign: University of Illinois, Center for the Study of Reading, April 1977.

SCHANK, R.C. "The Role of Memory in Language Processing," in C.N. Cofer (Ed.), *The Structure of Human Memory.* San Francisco: Freeman, 1977.

SHIMMERLIK, S.M. "Organization Theory and Memory for Prose; A Review of the Literature," *Review of Educational Research,* 48 (1978), 103–120.

SHIMMERLIK, S.M., and J.D. NOLAN. "Reorganization of the Recall of Prose," *Journal of Educational Psychology,* 68 (1976), 779–786.

SHORES, J.H. "Reading Comprehension in History and Science as Related to Reading and Study Skills," unpublished doctoral dissertation, University of Minnesota, 1940.

SIGAL, I.E. "The Attainment of Concepts," in M. Hoffman and L. Hoffman (Eds.), *Review of Child Development Research.* New York: Russell Sage Foundation, 1964.

SINGER, H. "Active Comprehension: From Answering to Asking Questions," *Reading Teacher,* 31 (May 1978), 901–908.

SMILEY, S.S., D.D. OAKLEY, D. WORTHEN, J.C. CAMPIONE, and A.L. BROWN. "Recall of Thematically Relevant Material by Adolescent Good and Poor Readers as a Function of Written versus Oral Presentation," *Journal of Educational Psychology,* 69 (1977), 381–387.

SMIRNOV, A.A., Z.M. ISTOMINA, K.P. MAL'TSEVA, and V.I. SAMOKHVALOVA. "The Development of Logical Memorization Techniques in the Preschool and Young School Child," *Soviet Psychology,* Winter 1971–1972, 178–195.

SMITH, H.K. "The Responses of Good and Poor Readers When Asked to Read for Different Purposes," *Reading Research Quarterly,* 1 (1967), 53–83.

SMITH, F. *Comprehension and Learning: A Conceptual Framework for Teachers.* New York: Holt, Rinehart and Winston, 1975.

SMITH, R.J., and T. BARRETT. *Teaching Reading in the Middle Grades.* Reading, Massachusetts: Addison-Wesley, 1974.

SNOWMAN, J., and D.J. CUNNINGHAM. "A Comparison of Pictorial and Written Adjunct Aids in Learning from Text," *Journal of Educational Psychology,* 67 (1975), 307–311.

SOCHOR, E. "Literal and Critical Reading in Social Studies," unpublished doctoral dissertation, Temple University, 1952.

SPACHE, G.D., and E.B. SPACHE. *Reading in the Elementary School* (Fourth Edition). Boston: Allyn and Bacon, 1977.

References   183

STAUFFER, R.G. *Teaching Reading as a Thinking Process.* New York: Harper and Row, 1969.

STAUFFER, R.G. *Directing the Reading-Thinking Process.* New York: Harper and Row, 1975.

STEIN, N.L. "The Effects of Increasing Temporal Disorganization on Children's Recall of Stories," paper presented at the Psychonomic Society Meetings, St. Louis, November 1976.

STEIN, N.L. "How Children Understand Stories: A Developmental Analysis," in L. Katz (Ed.), *Current Topics in Early Childhood Education* (Volume 2). Hillsdale, New Jersey: Ablex.

STEIN, N.L., and C.G. GLENN. "A Developmental Study of Children's Constructions of Stories," paper presented at the meeting of the Society for Research in Child Development, New Orleans, March 1977.

STEIN, N.L., and C.G. GLENN. "The Role of Structural Variation in Children's Recall of Simple Stories," paper presented at the meeting of the Society for Research in Child Development, New Orleans, March 1977.

STEIN, N.L., and C.G. GLENN. "An Analysis of Story Comprehension in Elementary School Children," in R. Freedle (Ed.), *Discourse Processing: Multidisciplinary Perspectives.* Hillsdale, New Jersey: Ablex, 1978.

STEIN, N.L., and T. NEZWORSKI. "The Effects of Organization and Instructional Set on Story Memory," *Discourse Processes,* 1 (1978), 177–194.

STEIN, N.L., and T. NEZWORSKI. "The Effects of Linguistic Markers on Children's Recall of Stories: A Developmental Study," unpublished manuscript, University of Illinois at Urbana-Champaign, 1977.

STRICKLAND, R. *The Language of Elementary School Children. Its Relationship to the Language of Reading Textbooks and the Quality of Reading of Selected Children,* Bulletin No. 38. Bloomington, Indiana: School of Education, Indiana University, 1962.

SULLIVAN, H.B. "A New Method of Determining Capacity for Reading," *Education,* 59 (1938), 39–45.

SURBER, C.F. "Developmental Processes in Social Inferences: Averaging of Intentions and Consequences in Moral Judgment," *Developmental Psychology,* 13 (1977), 654–665.

SUTTON-SMITH, B., G. BOTVIN, and D. MAHONEY. "Developmental Structures in Fantasy Narratives," *Human Development,* 19 (1976), 1–13.

SWABY, B. "The Effects of Advance Organizers and Vocabulary Introduction on the Reading Comprehension of Sixth Grade Students," unpublished dissertation, University of Minnesota, 1977.

SWENSON, E.J. "A Study of the Relationships among Various Types of Reading Scores on General and Science Materials," *Journal of Educational Research,* 36 (1942), 81–90.

TAYLOR, W.L. "Cloze Procedures: A New Tool for Measuring Readability," *Journalism Quarterly,* 30 (1953), 360–368.

THIEMAN, T.J., and W.F. BREWER. "Alfred Binet on Memory for Ideas," *Journal of Genetic Psychology*, 1978.

THIEMAN, T.J., and A.L. BROWN. *The Effects of Semantic and Formal Similarity on Recognition Memory for Sentence in Children*, Technical Report No. 76. Champaign: University of Illinois, Center for the Study of Reading, November 1977.

THORNDIKE, E.L. "The Psychology of Thinking in the Case of Reading," *Psychological Review*, 24 (1917a), 220–234.

THORNDIKE, E.L. "Reading as Reasoning: A Study of Mistakes in Paragraph Reading," *Elementary School Journal*, 8 (1917b), 98–114.

THORNDYKE, P.W. "Cognitive Structures in Comprehension and Memory of Narrative Discourse," *Cognitive Psychology*, 9 (1977), 77–110.

TRABASSO, T., and D.W. NICHOLAS. "Memory and Inferences in the Comprehension of Narratives," paper presented at a conference on Structure and Process Models in the Study of Dimensionality of Children's Judgements, Kassel, Germany, June 1977.

TRIPLETT, D.G. "A Test of Two Prose Learning Strategies: Imagery and Paraphrase," unpublished doctoral dissertation, University of Wisconsin at Madison, 1980.

TUINMAN, J.J. "Determining the Passage Dependency of Comprehension Questions in Five Major Tests," *Reading Research Quarterly*, 9 (1973–1974), 206–223.

TYLER, R.W. "Measuring the Ability to Infer," *Educational Research Bulletin*, 9 (1930), 475–480.

WARREN, W.H., D.W. NICHOLAS, and T. TRABASSO. "Event Chains and Inferences in Understanding Narratives," in R.O. Freedle (Ed.), *Discourse Processing: Multidisciplinary Approaches*. Hillsdale, New Jersey: Erlbaum, 1978.

WATTS, G.H. "The 'Arousal' Effect of Adjunct Questions on Recall from Prose Materials," *Australian Journal of Psychology*, 25 (1973), 81–87.

WATTS, G.H., and E.C. ANDERSON. "Effects of Three Types of Inserted Questions on Learning from Prose," *Journal of Educational Psychology*, 62 (1971), 387–394.

WEINSTEIN, C.E., et al. "Cognitive Learning Strategies: Verbal and Imaginal Elaboration," in H.F. O'Neill, Jr. and C.D. Spielberger (Eds.), *Cognitive and Affective Learning Strategies*. New York: Academic Press, 1979.

WEISBERG, R. "A Comparison of Good and Poor Readers' Ability to Comprehend Implicit Information in Short Stories Based on Two Modes of Presentation," unpublished doctoral dissertation, Temple University, 1978.

WERTSCH, J.V. "Adult-Child Interaction and the Roots of Metacognition," *Quarterly Newsletter of the Institute for Comparative Human Development*, 2 (1978), 15–18.

References

185

WILKIE, E.B. *A Trial of Materials Designed to Improve Readers' Comprehension Skills,* Working Paper No. 230. Madison: Wisconsin Research and Development Center for Individualized Schooling, 1978.

WIMMER, H. "Children's Comprehension and Recall of Hierarchically Structured Stories," paper presented at the meeting of the Society for Research in Child Development, San Francisco, March 1979.

YENDOVITSKAYZ, T.V. "Development of Memory," in A.V. Zaporszhets and D.B. Elkonin (Eds.), *The Psychology of Preschool Children.* Cambridge, Massachusetts: MIT Press, 1971.

YOST, M., L. AVILA, and E.B. VEXLER. "Effect on Learning of Postinstructional Responses to Questions of Differing Degrees of Complexity," *Journal of Educational Psychology,* 69 (1977), 399–408.

YOUNG, W.E. "The Relation of Comprehension and Retention in Reading to Comprehension and Retention in Hearing," unpublished doctoral dissertation, University of Iowa, 1930.

ZINTZ, M.F. *The Reading Process.* Dubuque, Iowa: Wm. C. Brown, 1970.